Classic American Mistress

Volume Two

Goddess Jude

David Sawyer

CAM Publishing
PO Box 522
Milford, CT 06460

INTRODUCTION

Welcome to Volume Two of *Classic American Mistress.* In this edition we are proud to present Goddess Jude of Orlando, Florida. Goddess Jude is a skilled professional dominatrix that utilizes all the fine arts of B&D and has been practicing them for several years in her private studio. Those wishing to contact her about a private session can write to goddessjude@gmail.com

In this volume of *Classic American Mistress,* we offer a wide range of color photos that capture Goddess Jude in many different outfits for her many different moods. We are confident you will be captivated by her beauty and power. Well will now step into the sensuous world of Goddess Jude!

Enjoy!

David Sawyer
(1-3-15)

Goddess Jude

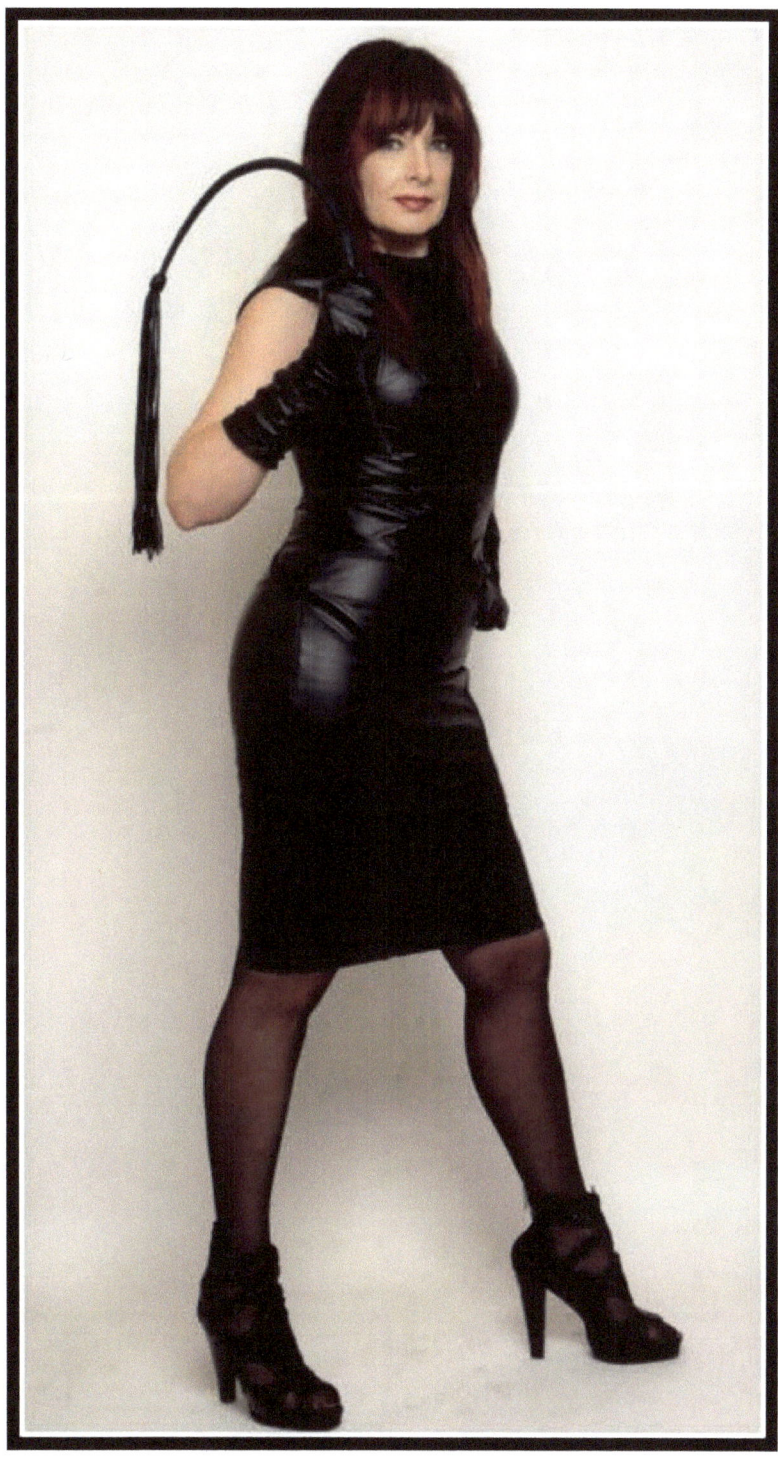

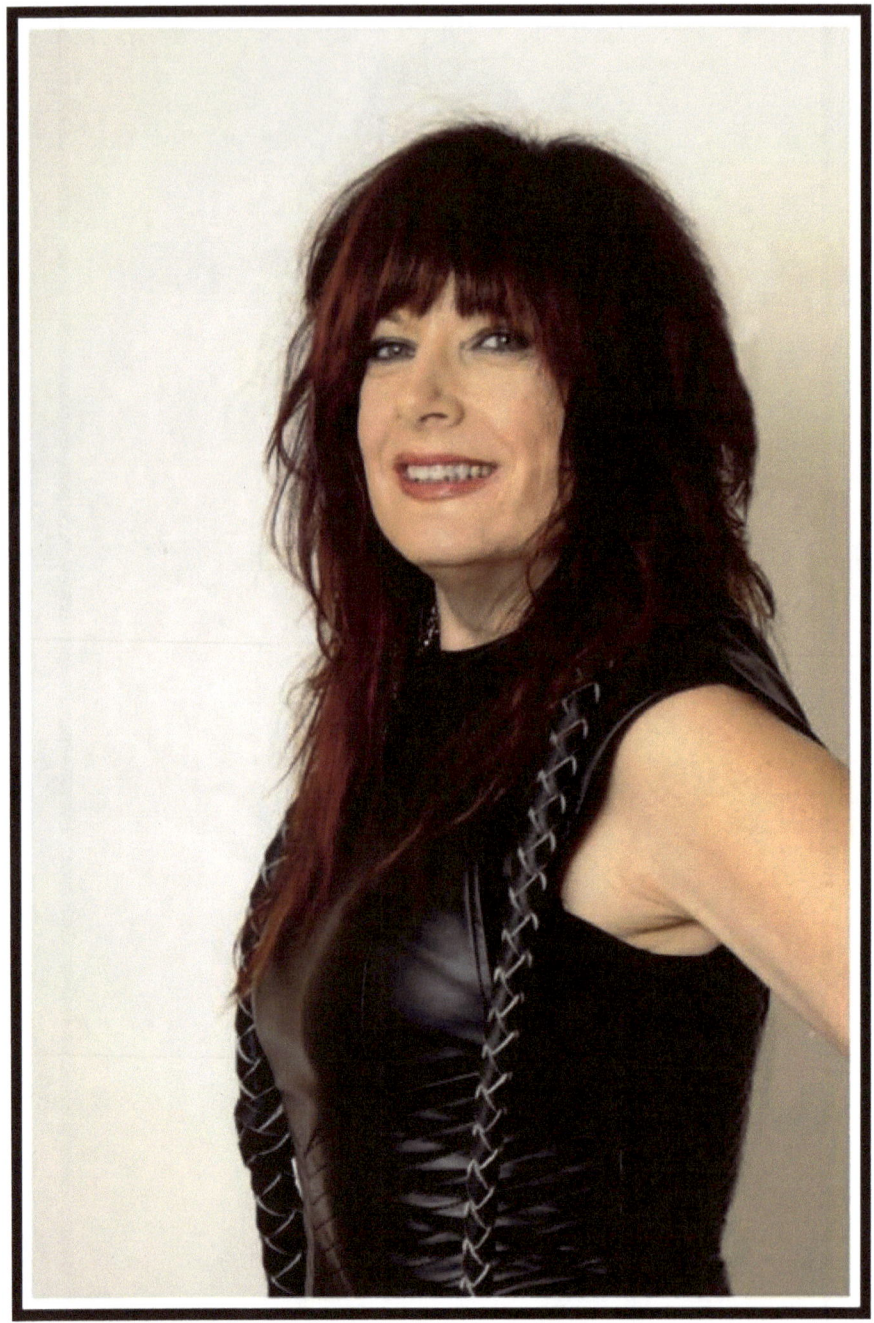

(Goddess Jude from a 2014 photo shoot)

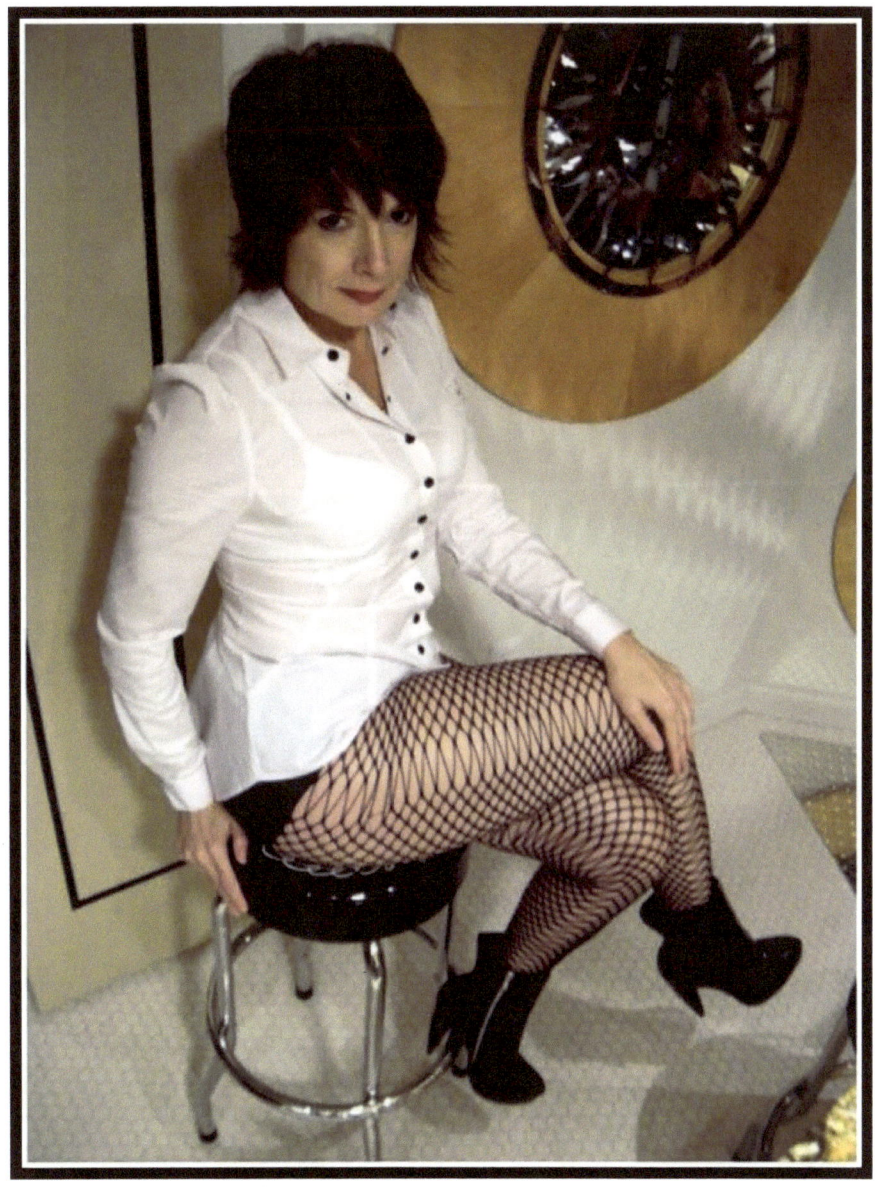

(Goddess Jude in 2010 with her shorter hairstyle and fishnet stockings)

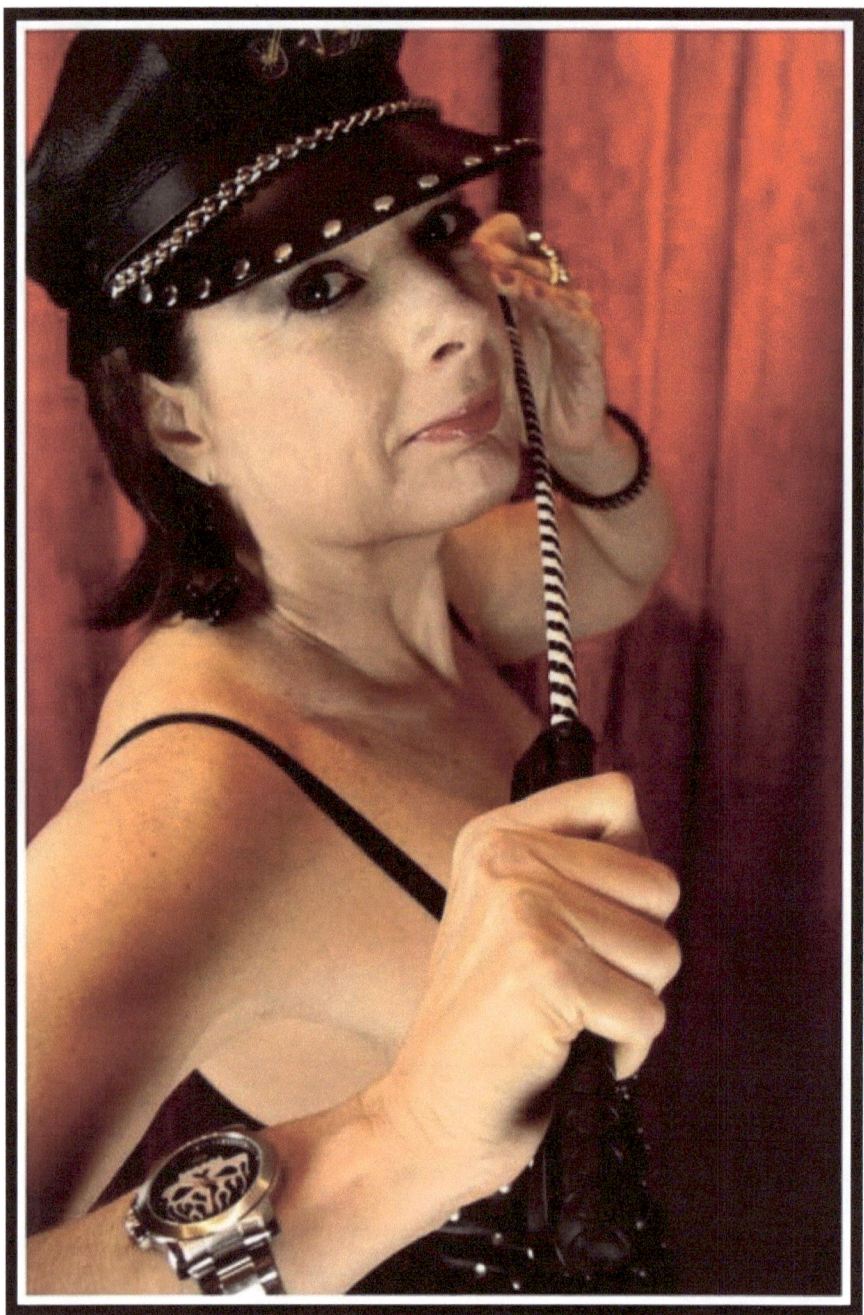

(Goddess Jude in 2011)

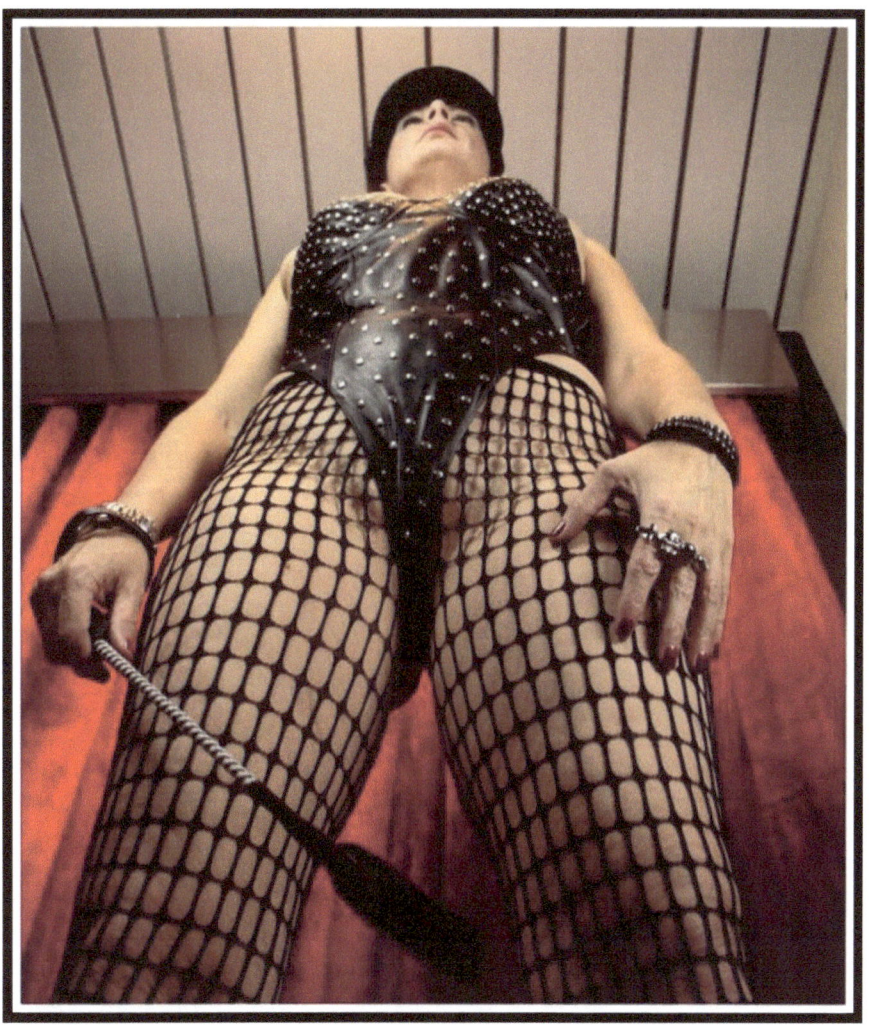

Goddess Jude can contacted for private session through her website goddessjude.com

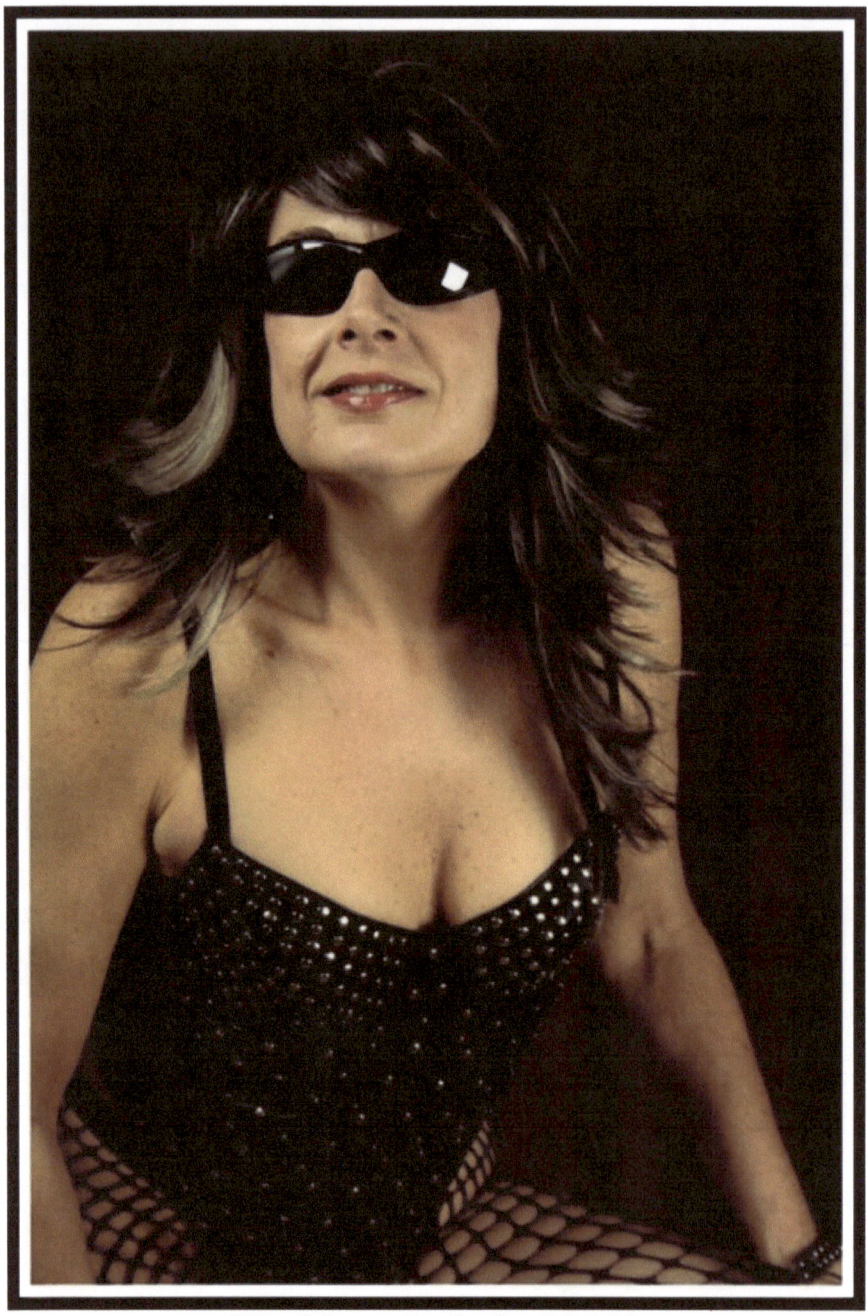

(Goddess Jude in 2011)

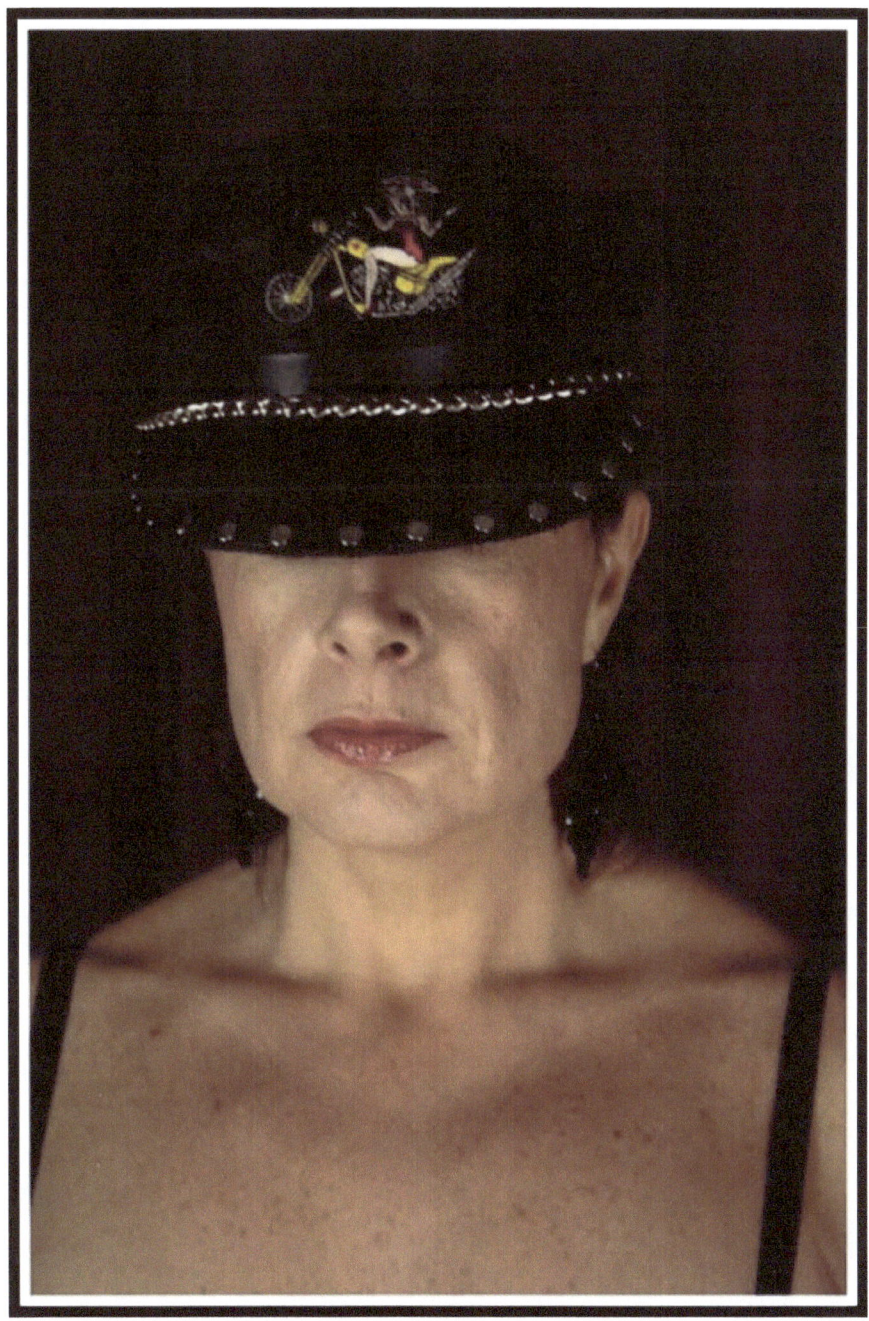

(Goddess Jude 2011)

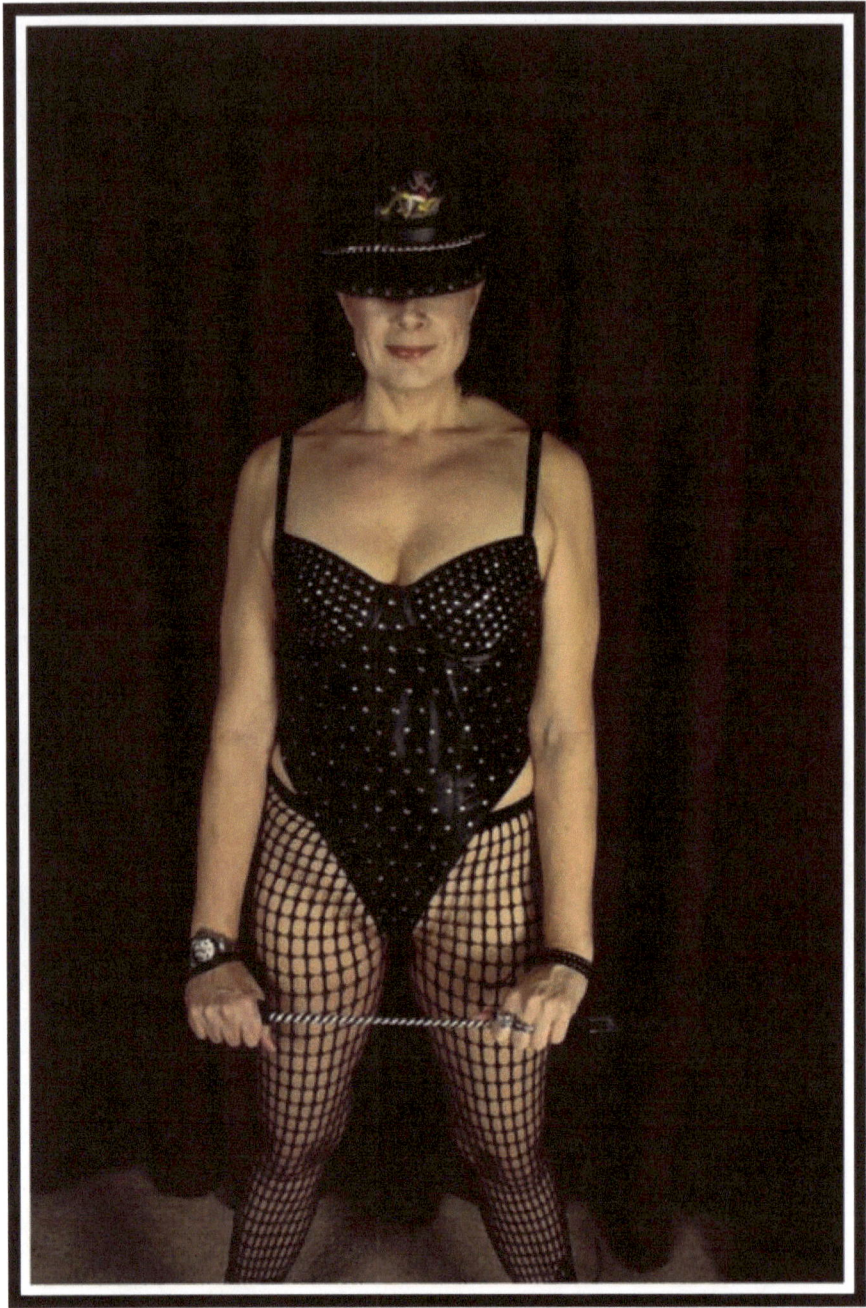

(Goddess Jude in command in 2011)

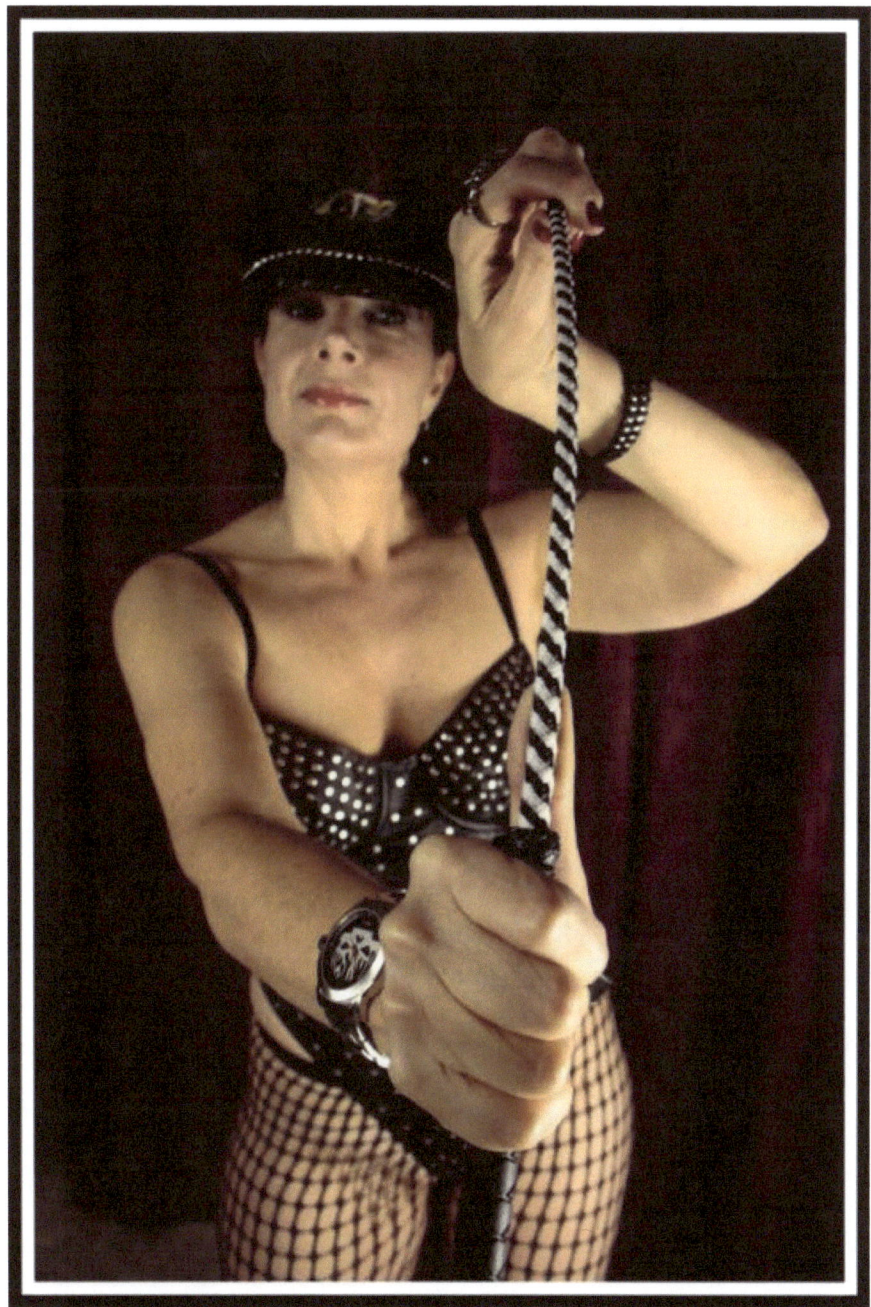

(Goddess Jude cracks her whip in 2011)

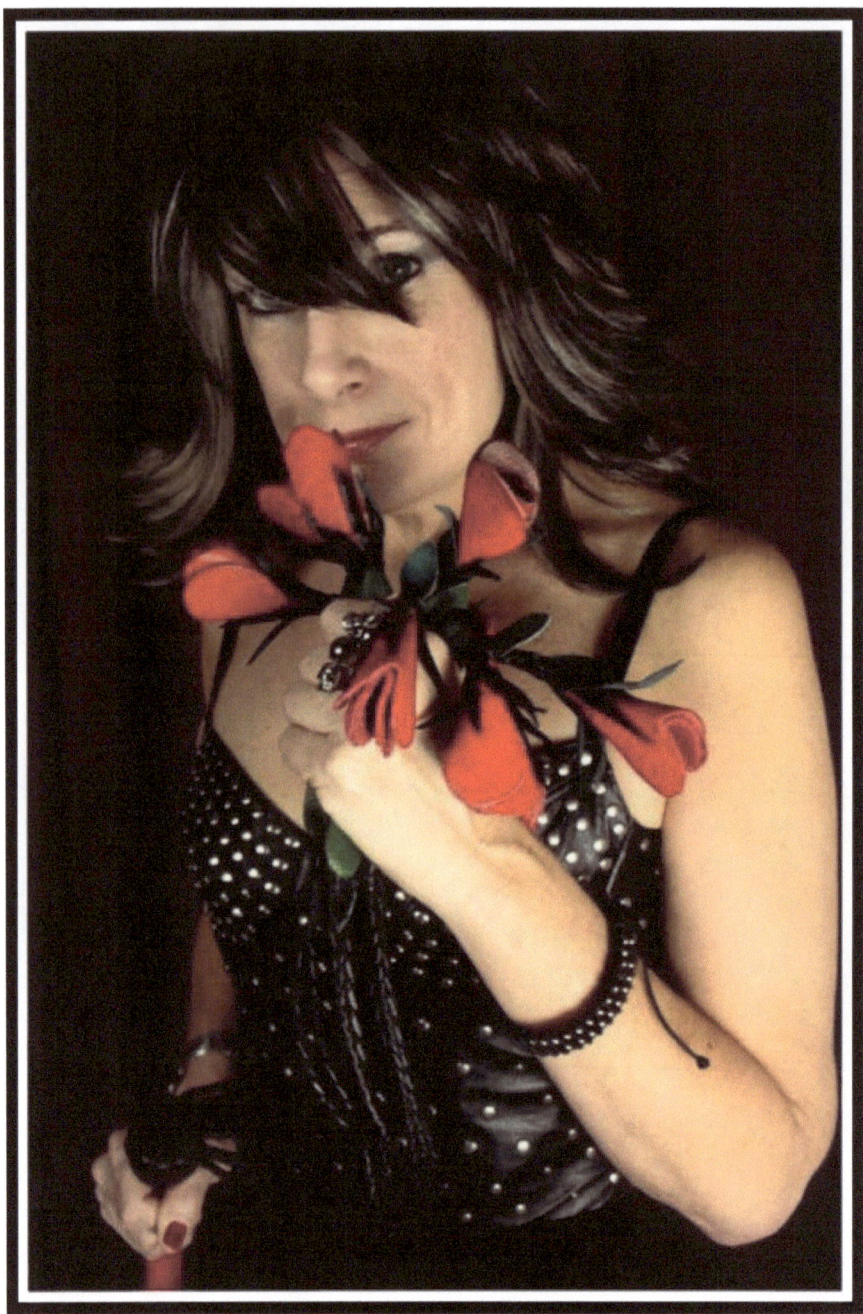

goddessjude.com

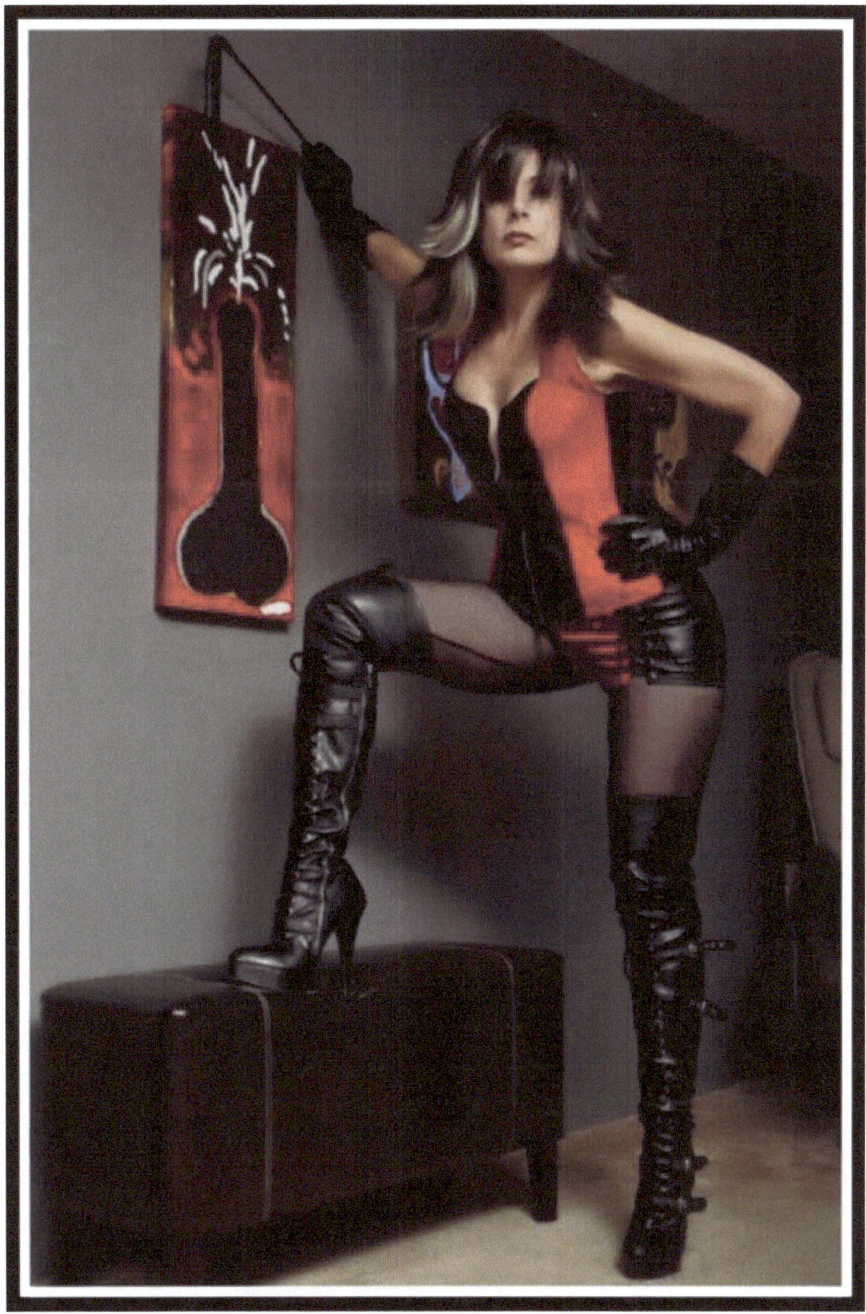

(Goddess Jude in 2012)

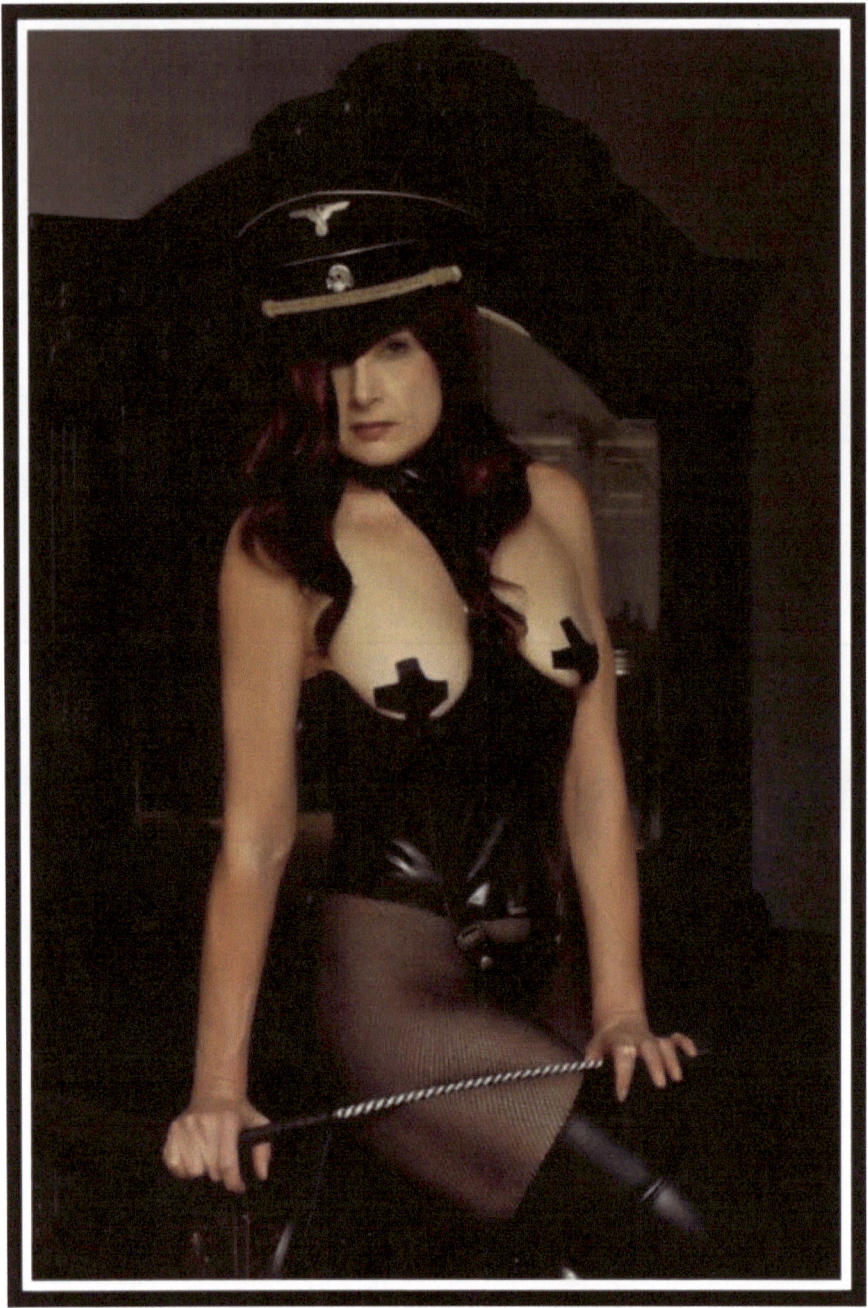

(Goddess Jude in 2012)

Goddess Jude

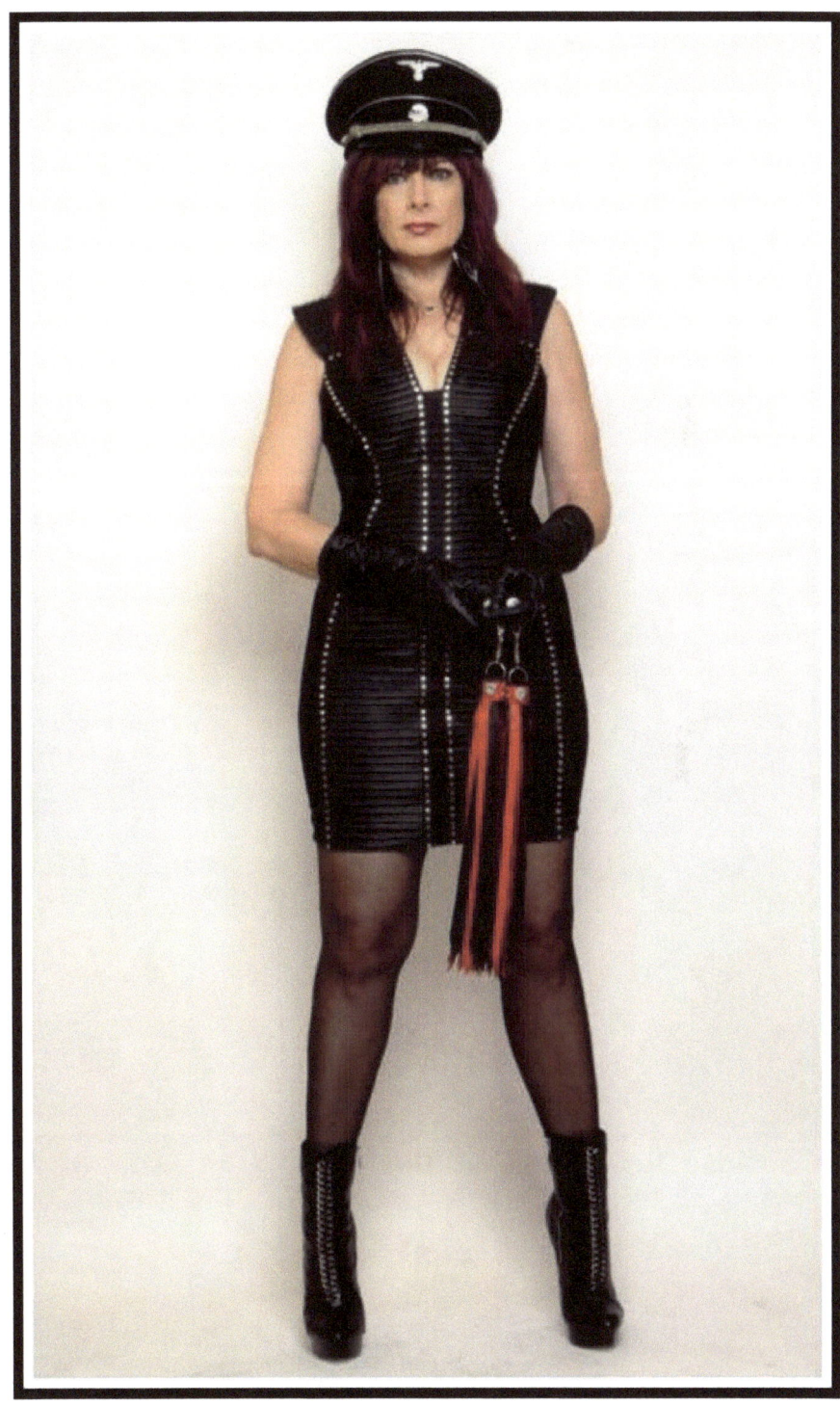

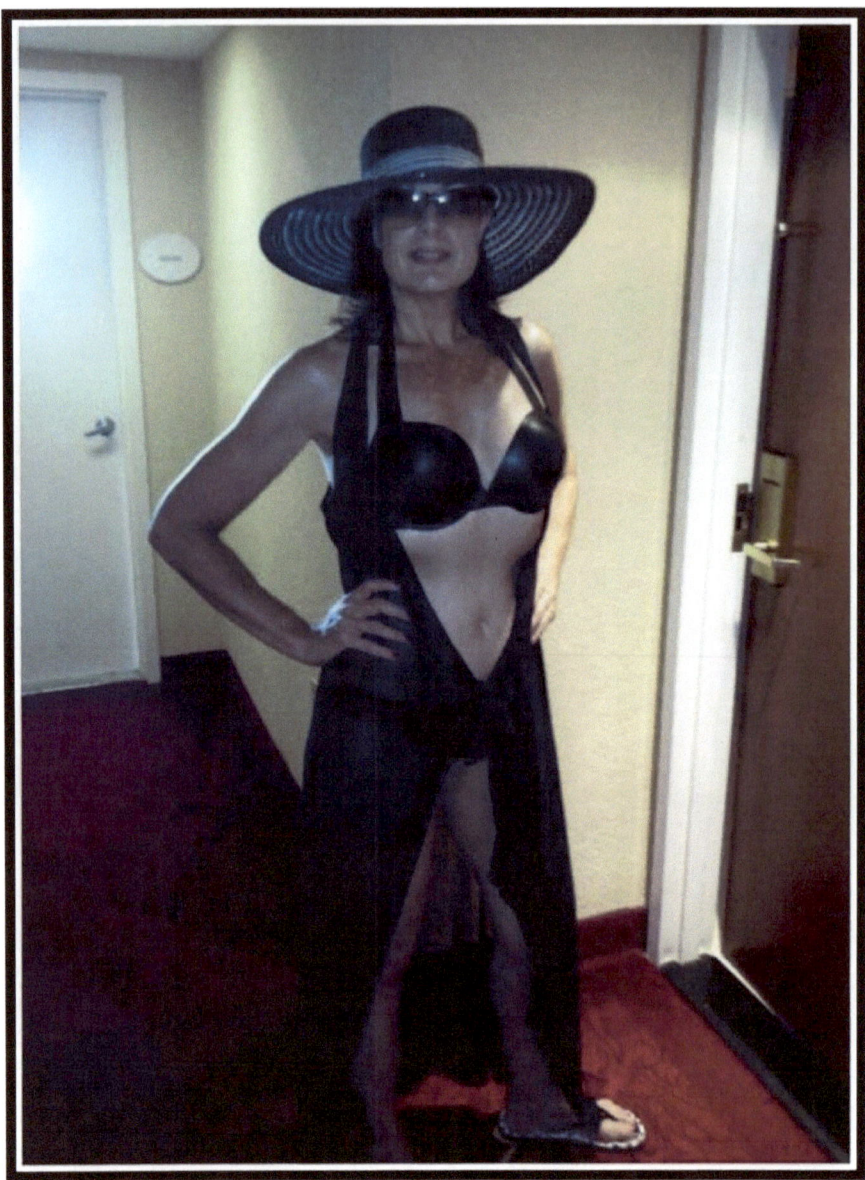

(Goddess Jude back from the beach in 2012 and looking absolutely devastating in a black bikini!)

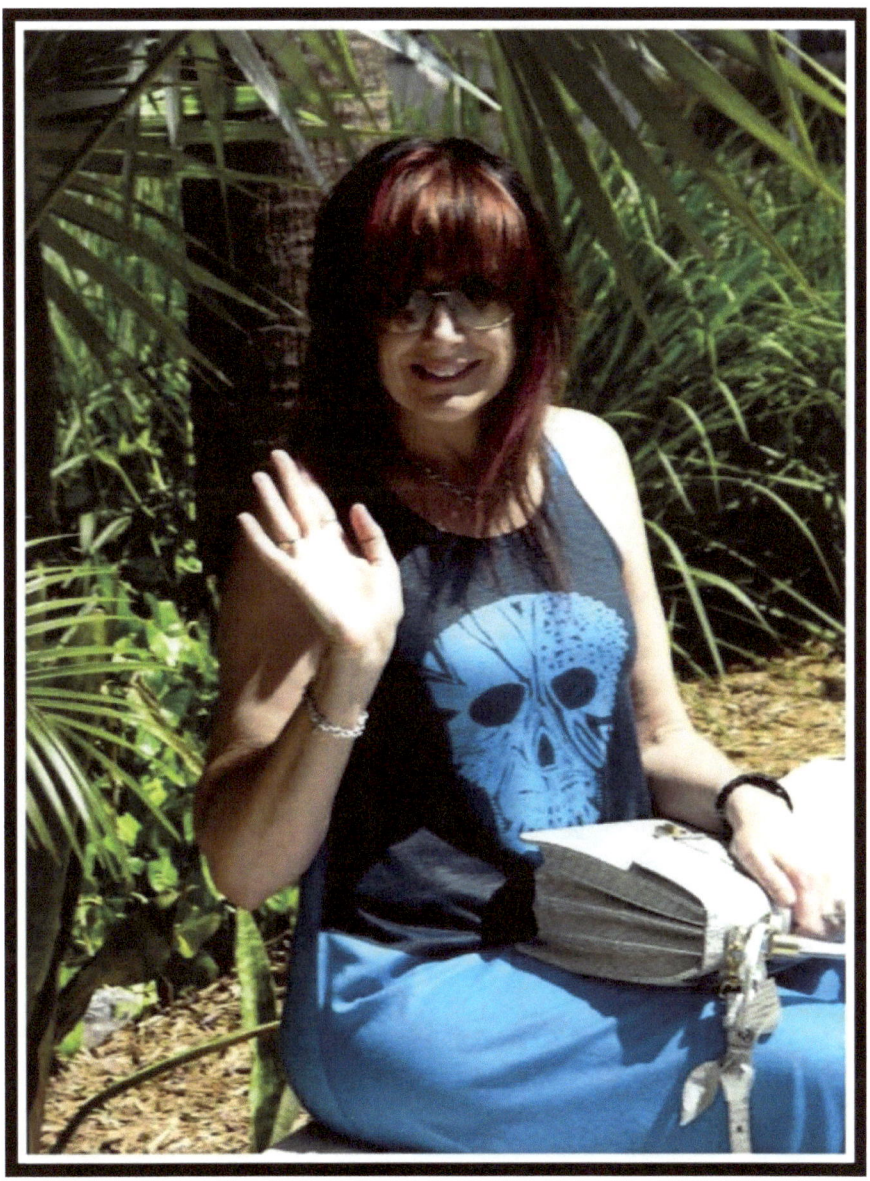

(Goddess Jude enjoying the sun in Key West, Florida)

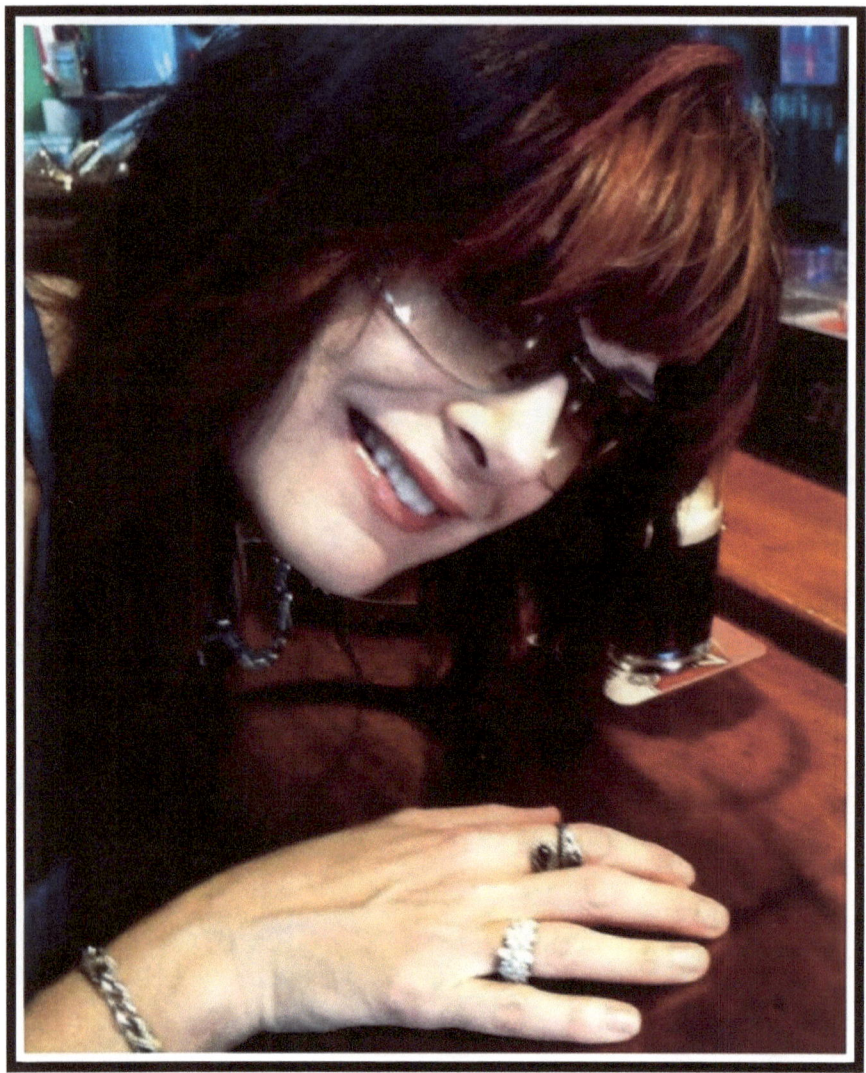

(Goddess Jude out on the town in Key West, Florida)

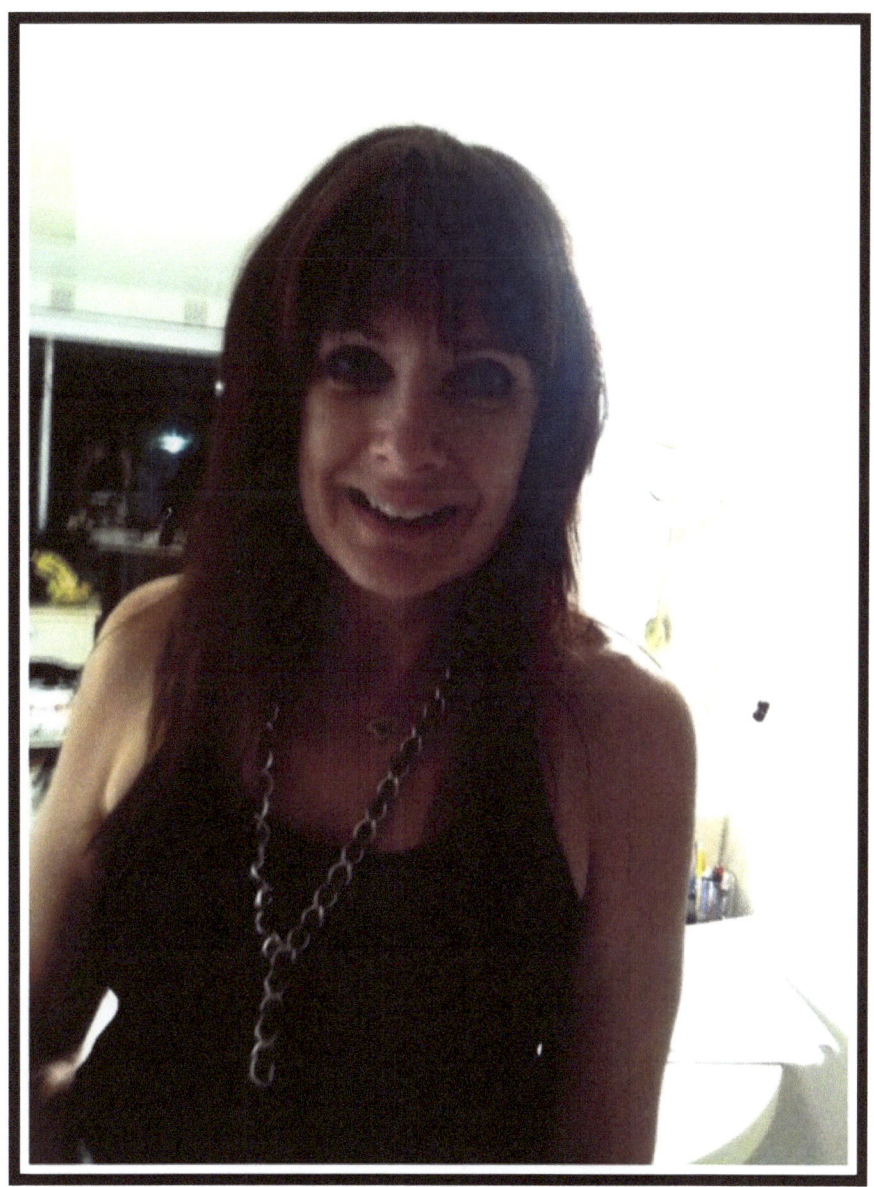

(Goddess Jude in 2014)

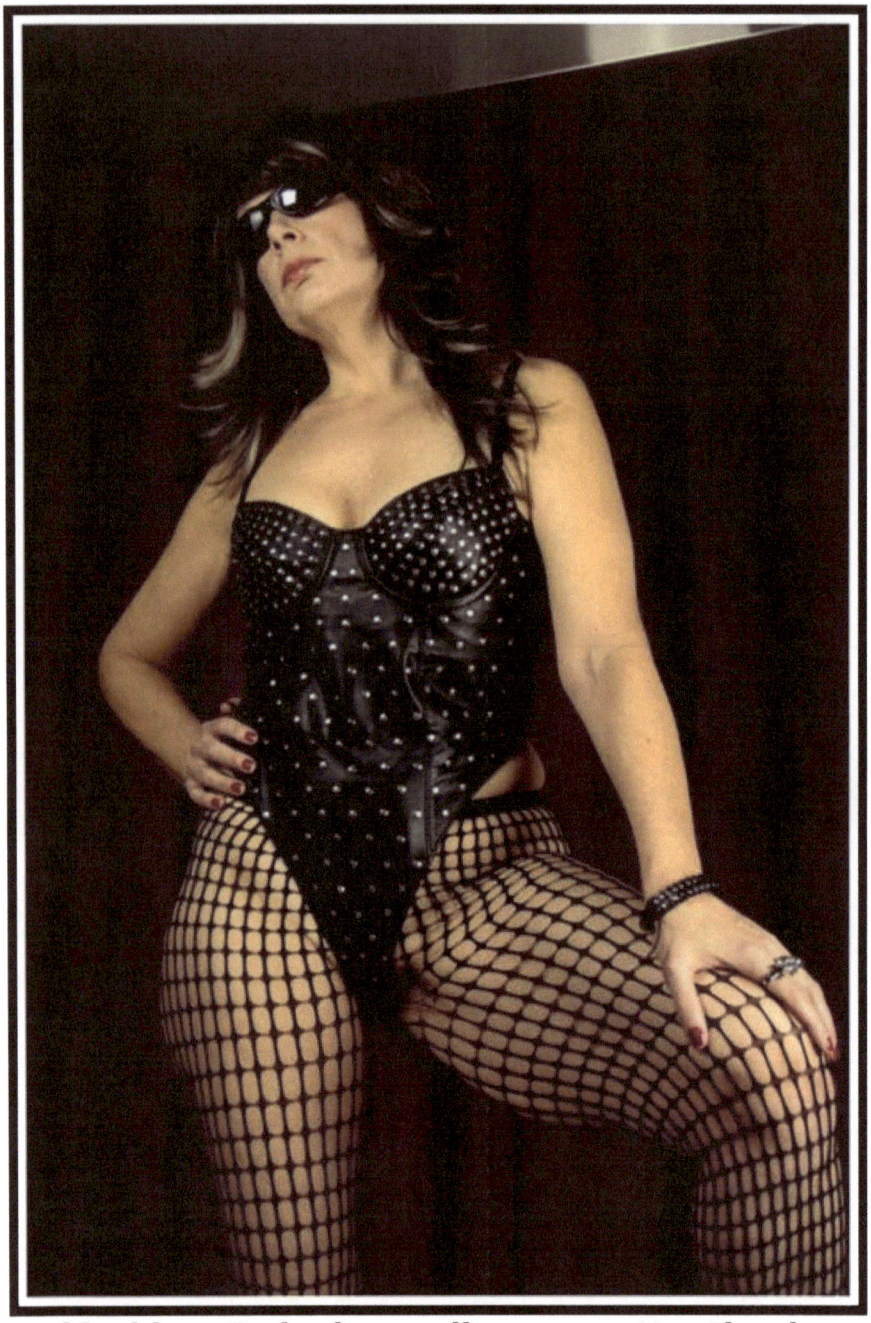

(Goddess Jude demanding your attention in 2011)

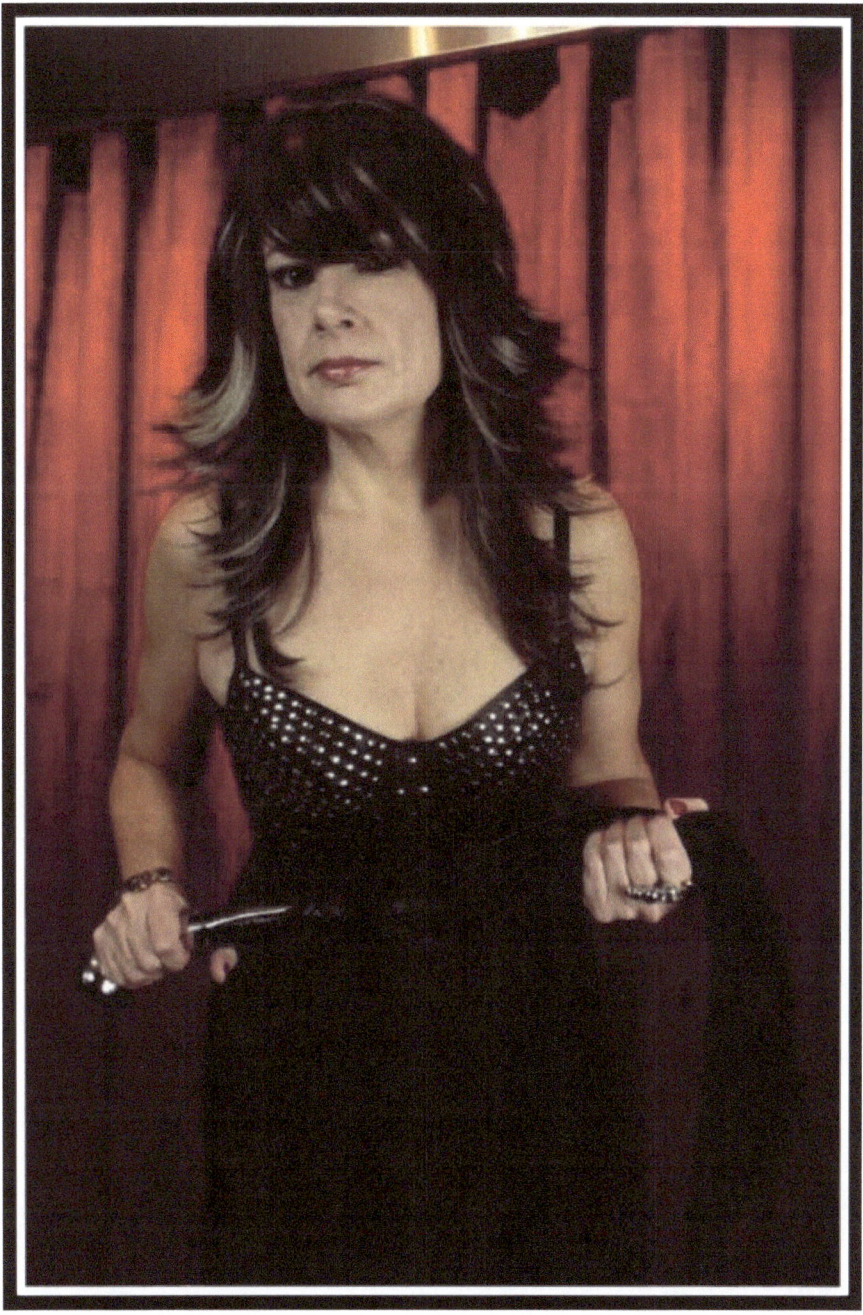

(Visit Goddess Jude at goddessjude.com)

Goddess Jude In Her Own Words

I was interested with the world of fetish and goth before I got into BDSM. The event that pointed me into the direction I am in today was the Fetish Factory 14th Anniversary weekend in May of 2009. From that point forward I got into more BDSM events in the Tampa and Fort Lauderdale area.

I fell in love with the dominatrix look and demeanor, I picked up the Domme role as if it was second nature. After the Fetish Factory 14th Anniversary weekend, I decided to give the pro-Domme thing a go and Goddess Jude was born.

The last weekend of July 2010 I ran an ad on a low budget national internet website in Daytona Beach (which is 45 minutes from my home in Orlando.) I began to offer domination sessions and I began to get more practice. I booked a few clients for one day and I absolutely loved every second of it. I quickly got rave reviews, including one from a client who said I was the best Domme he had served in 20 years. None of my early clients seemed to have any idea that I was a beginner.

I love the psychological aspects of BDSM, the attitude and of course the edgy look. I got so much pleasure out of dominating and I received a decent income for my emerging skills that I just had to move forward. I ran my ad again in my home town of Orlando and I officially joined the Mistress business in September of 2010.

I have since seen many slaves, submissives and even couples from all over the world. I have a wonderfully loyal following and continue to meets new folks all the time. I am a very happy being a professional dominatrix and I wouldn't trade what I do for the world!

Goddess Jude
Orlando, Florida
1-4-15

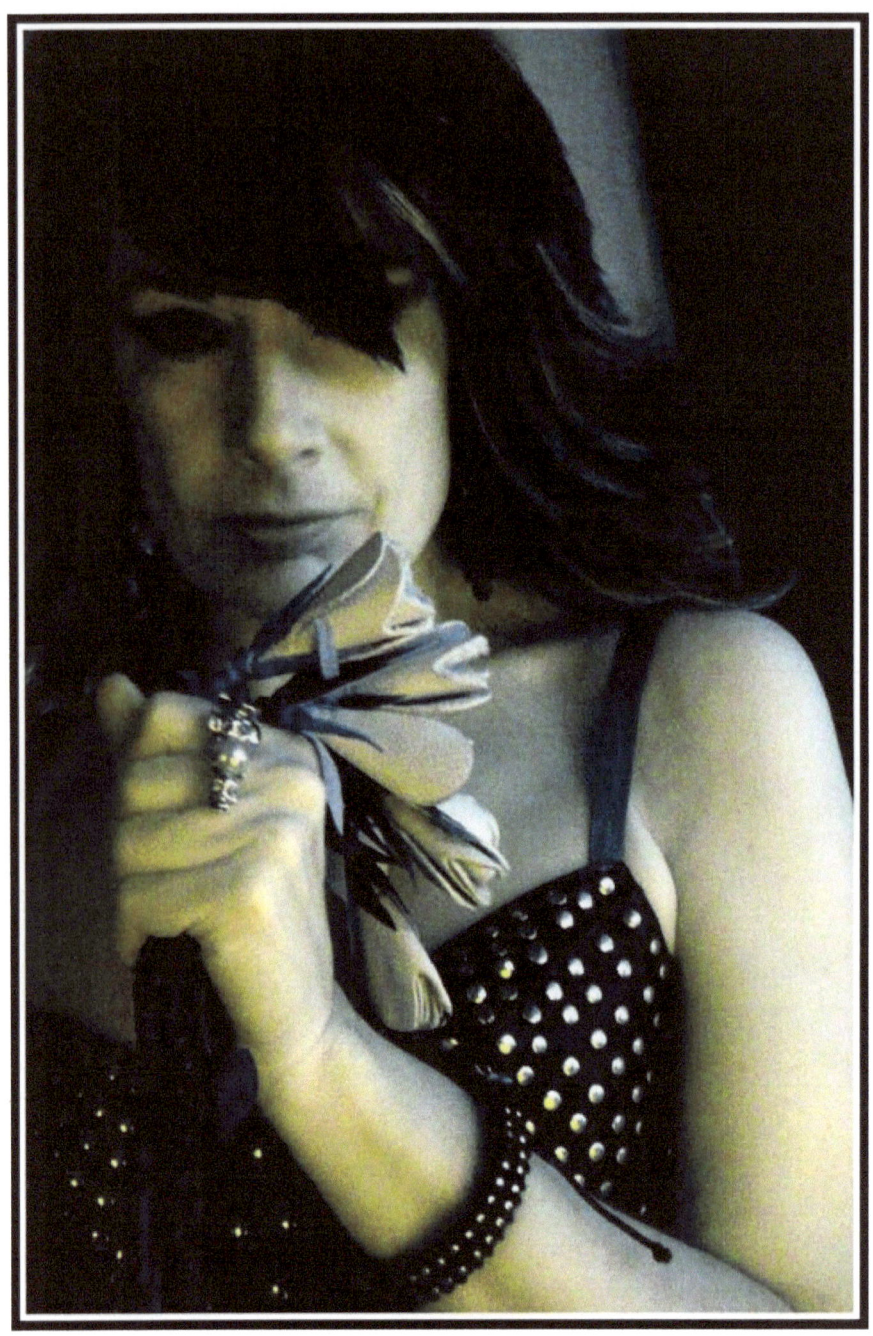

(Goddess Jude 2011)

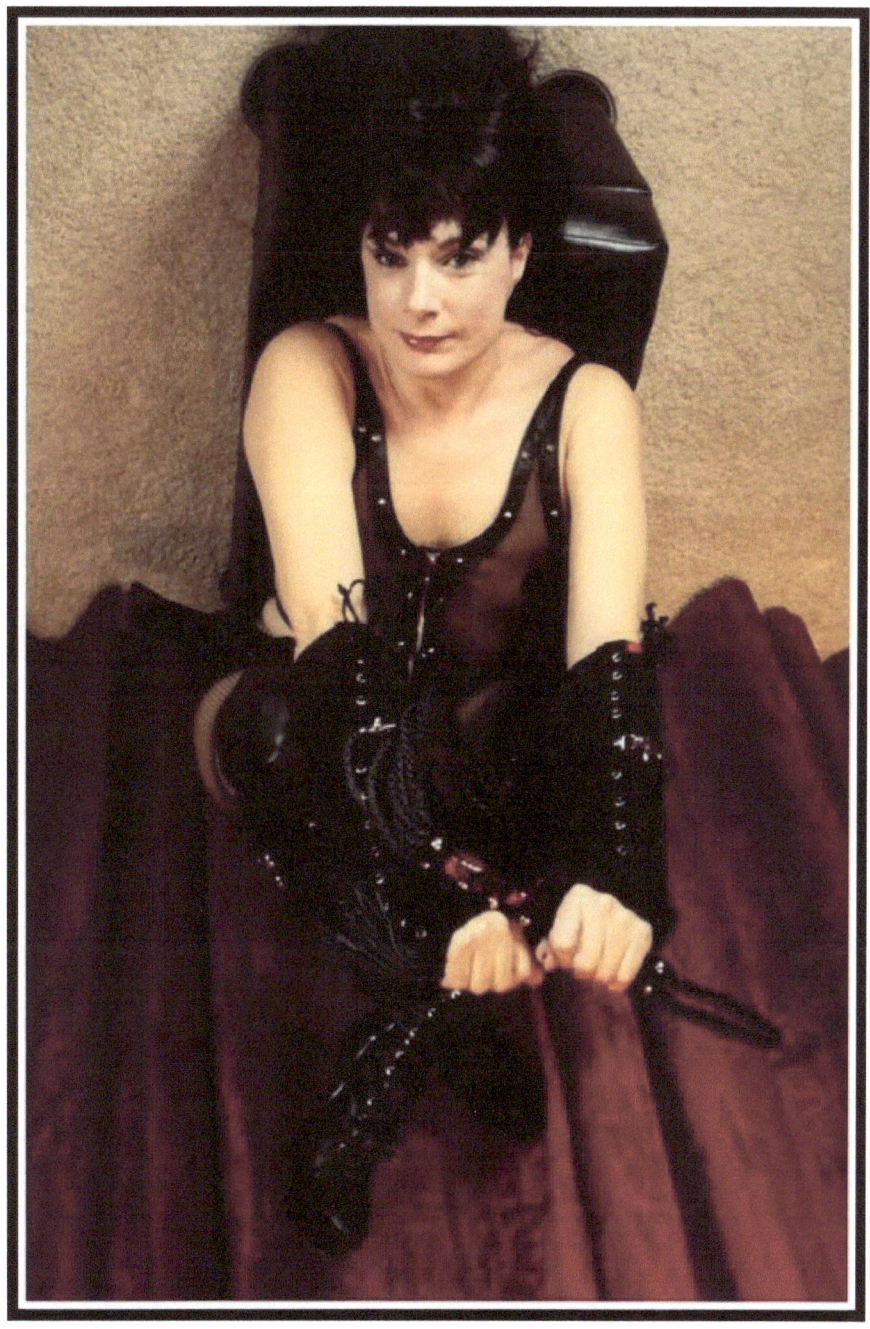

(Goddess Jude 2011)

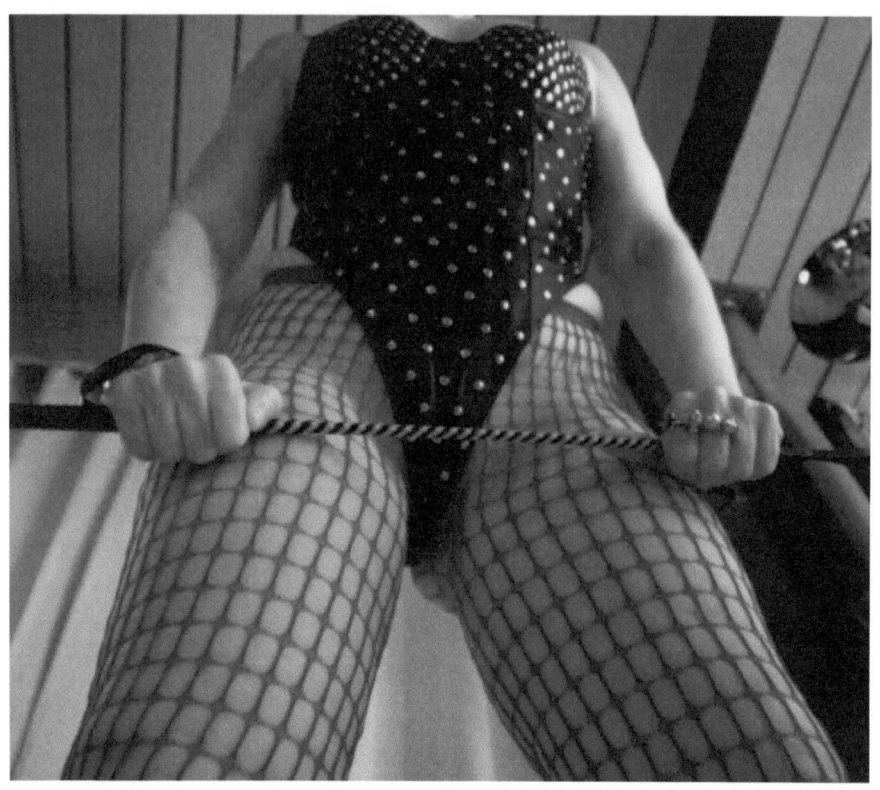

Goddess Jude's Special Interests

Abandonment
Candle Wax Play
CBT
Cross Dressing
Electro Play (including violet wand)
Flogging
Foot Worship
Role Play
Sissy Training
Sounding
Spanking
Whipping
and more!!!!!

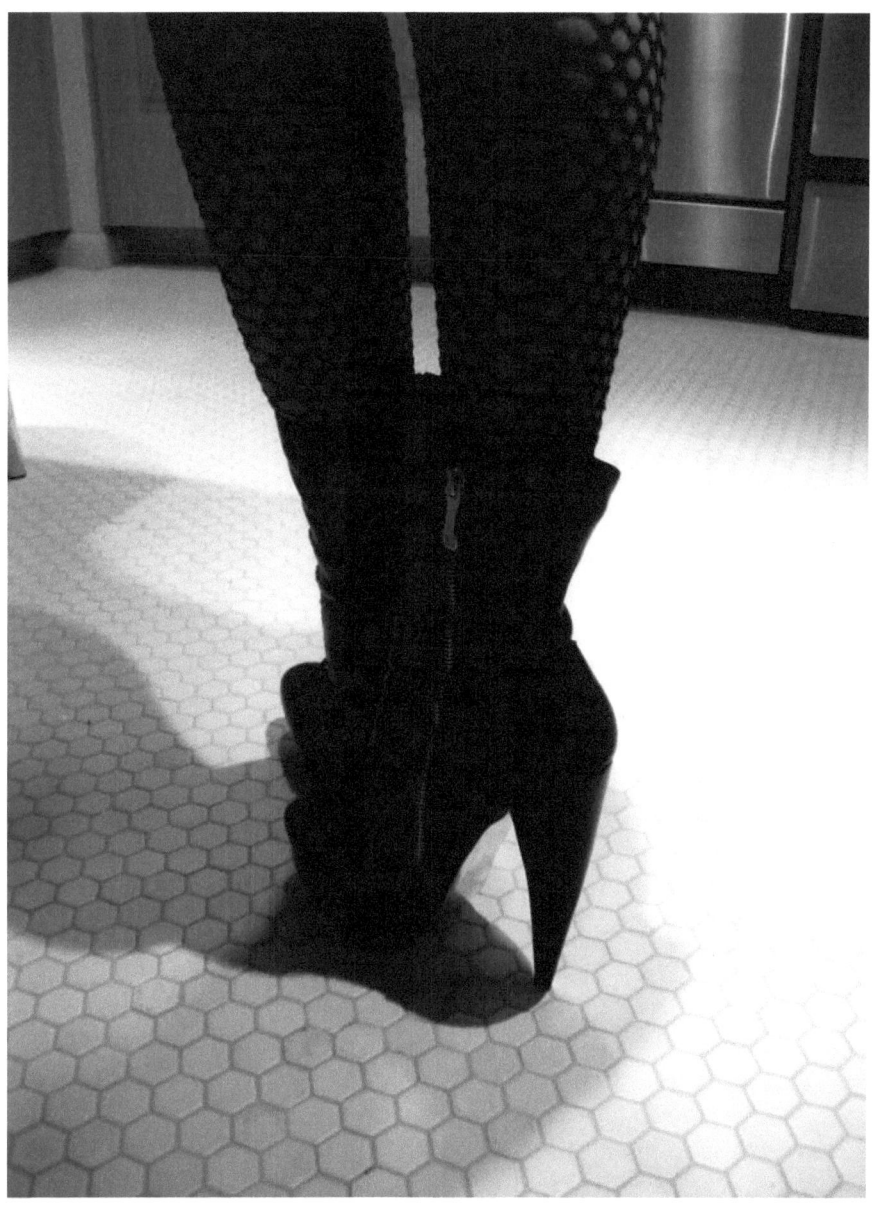

(Goddess Jude 2010)

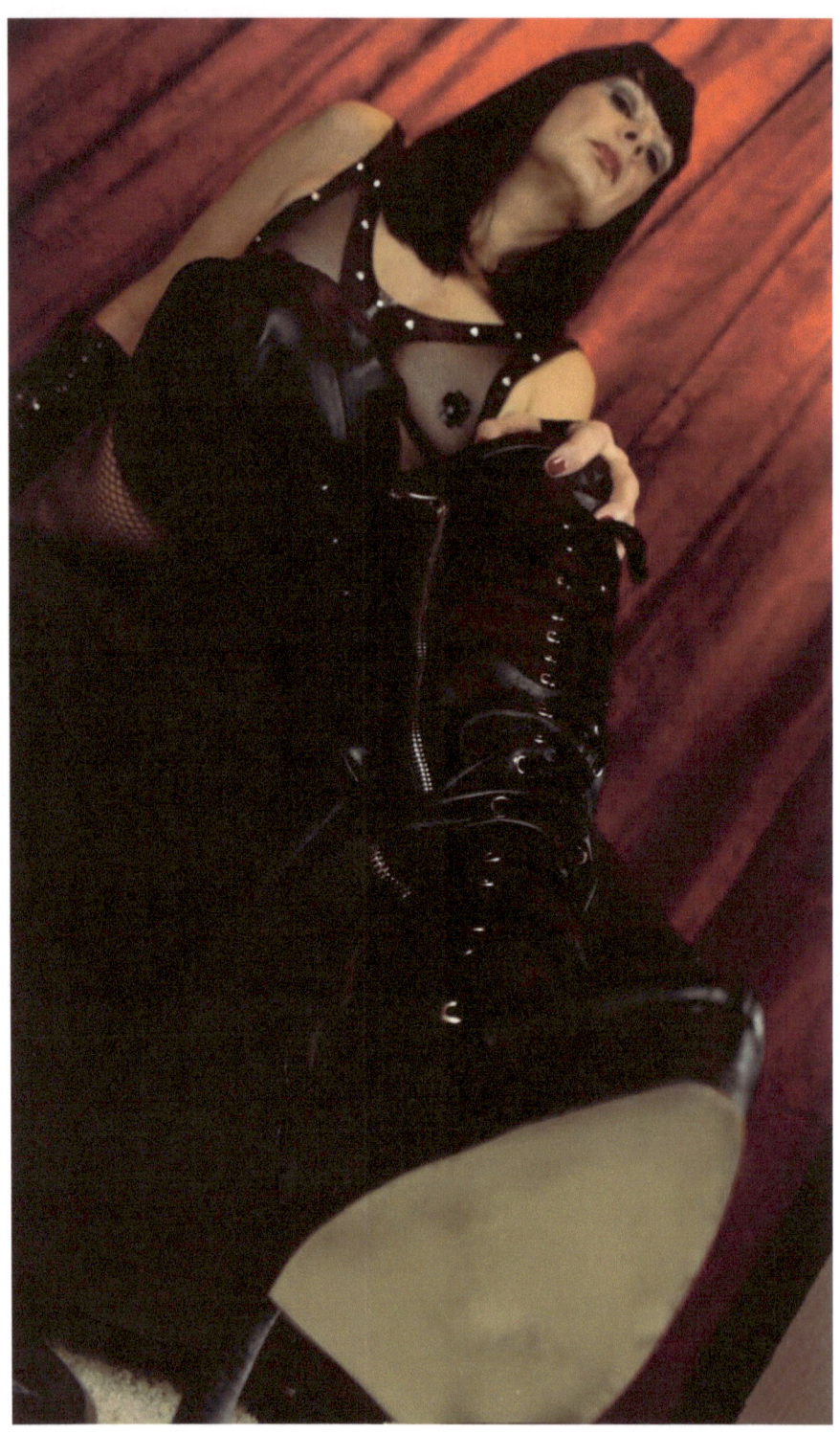

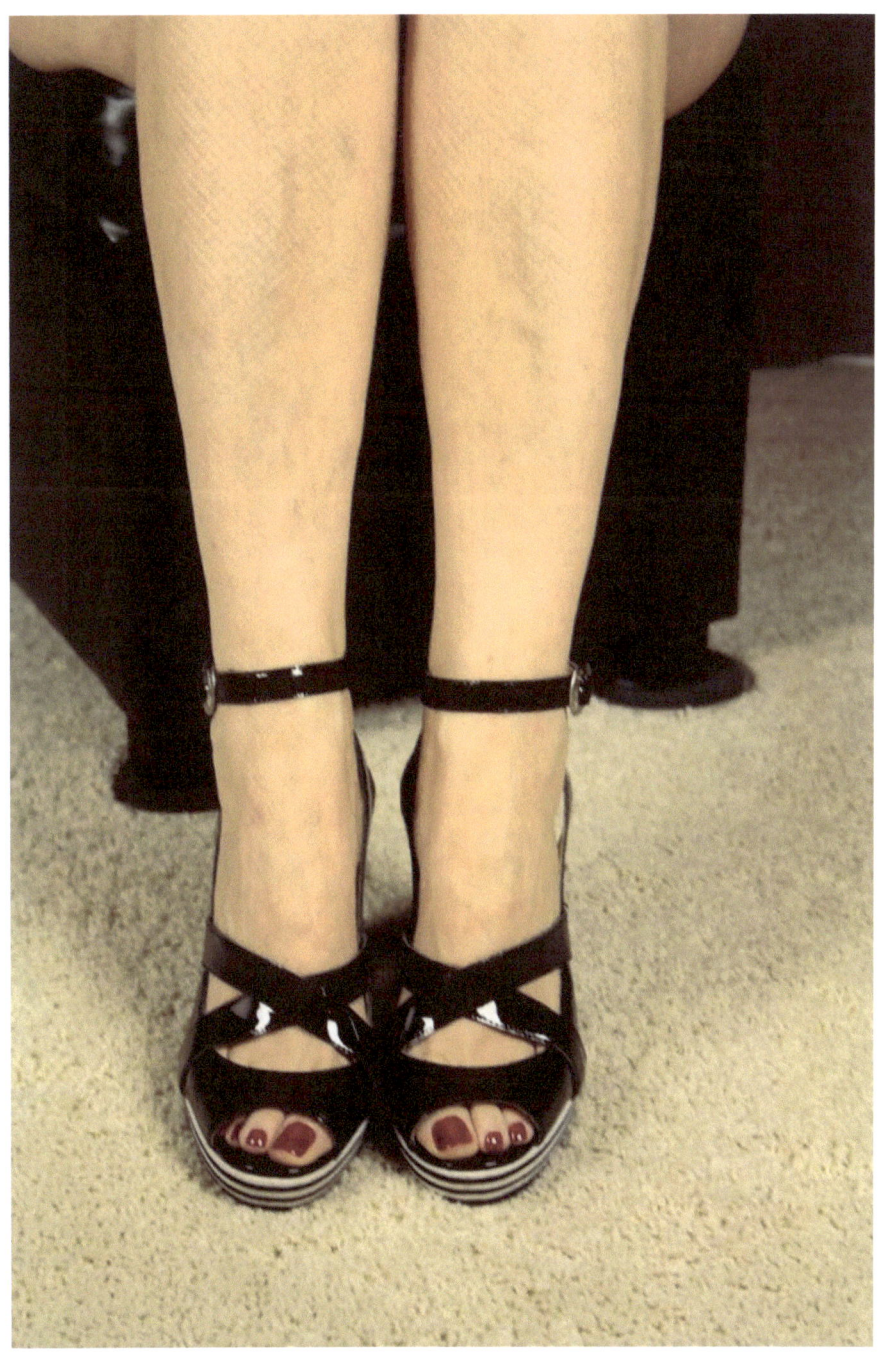

(Goddess Jude 2011)

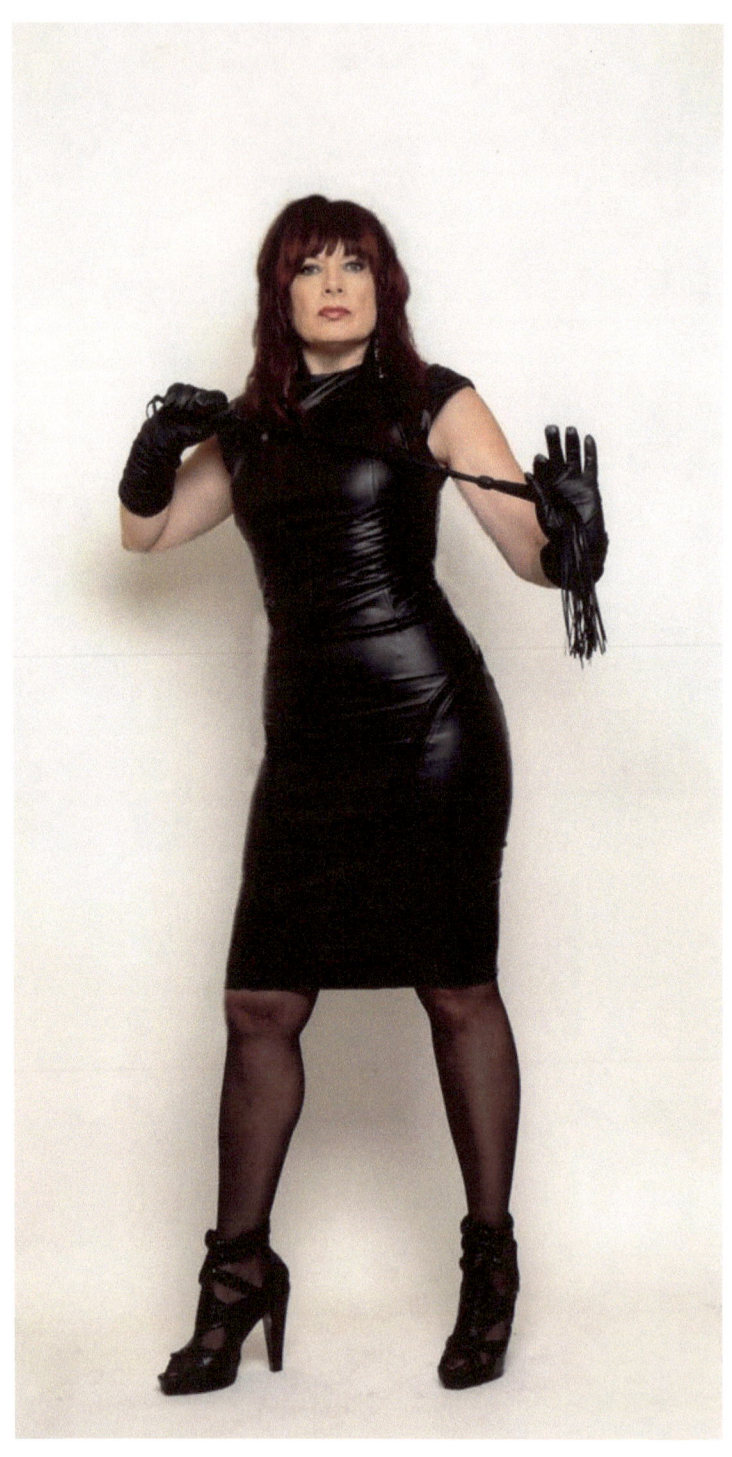

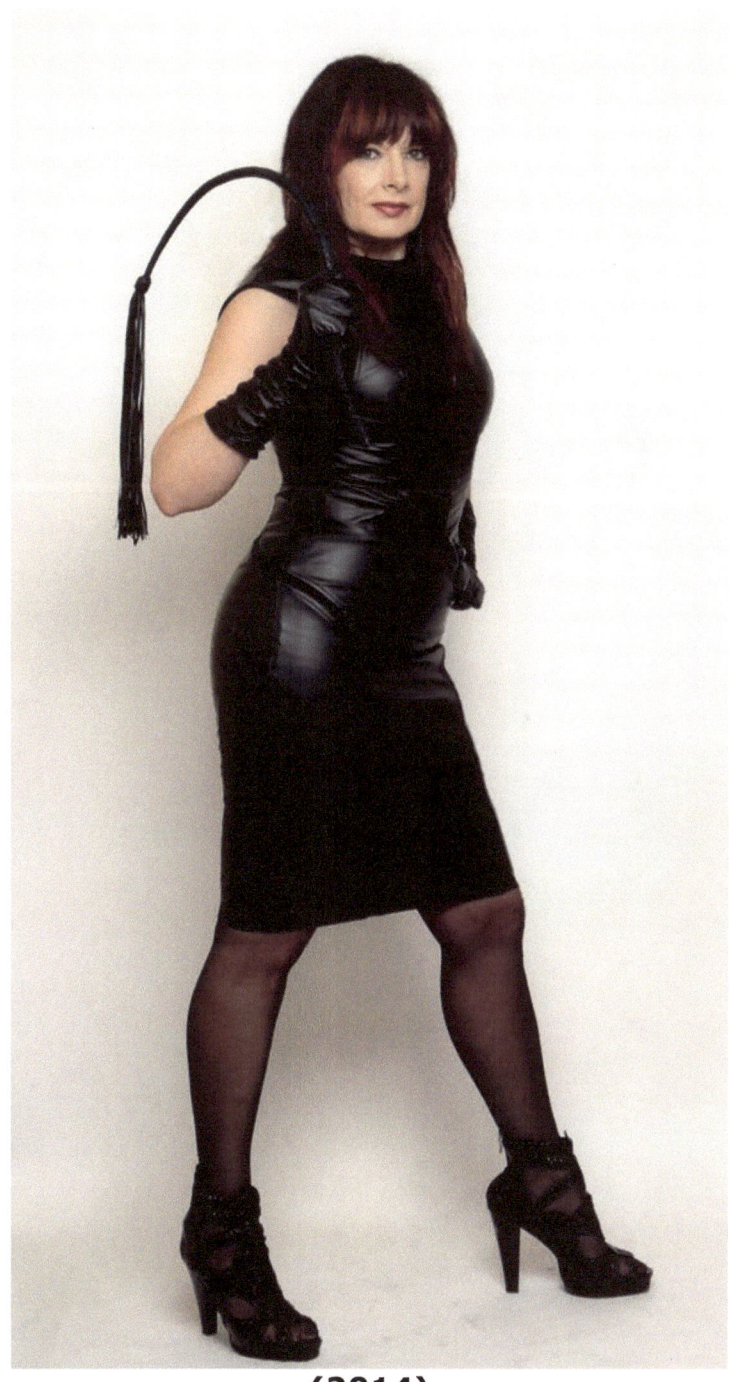

(2014)

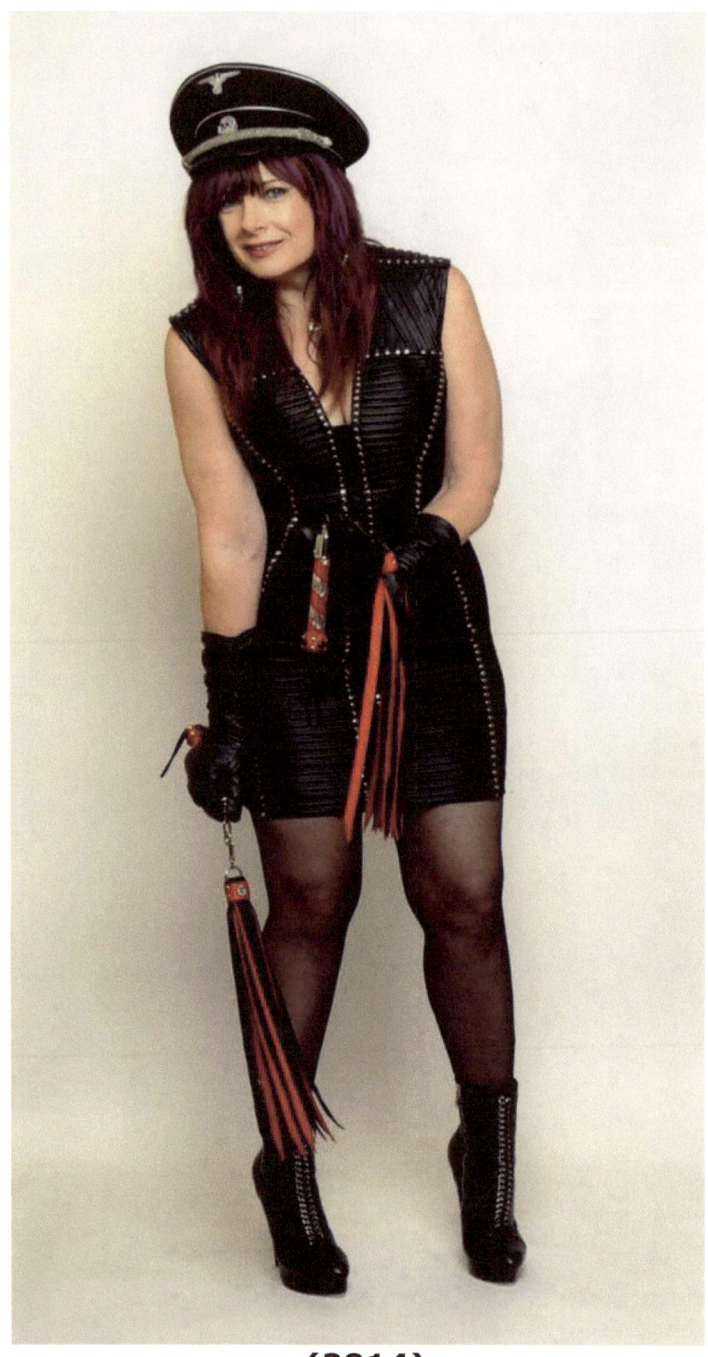

(2014)

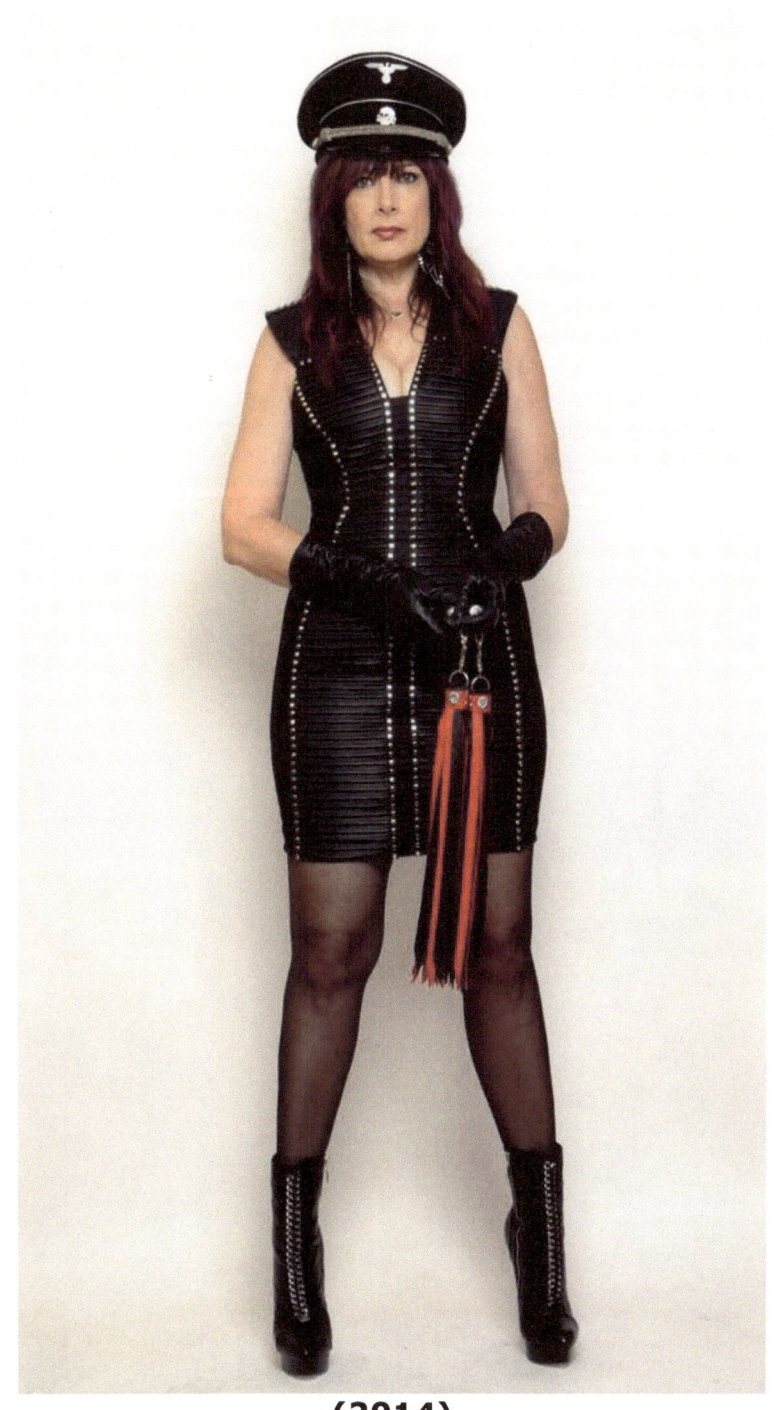

(2014)

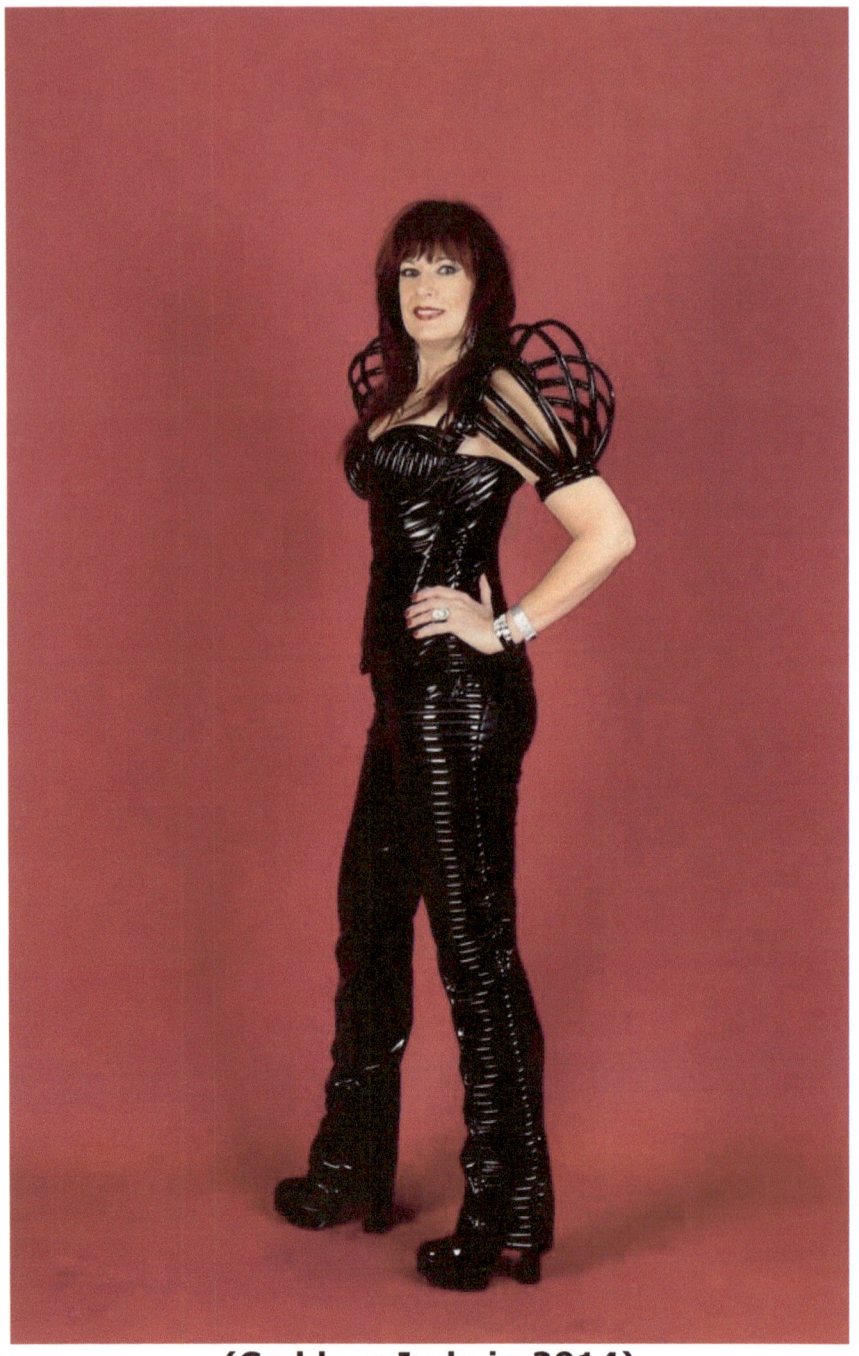

(Goddess Jude in 2014)

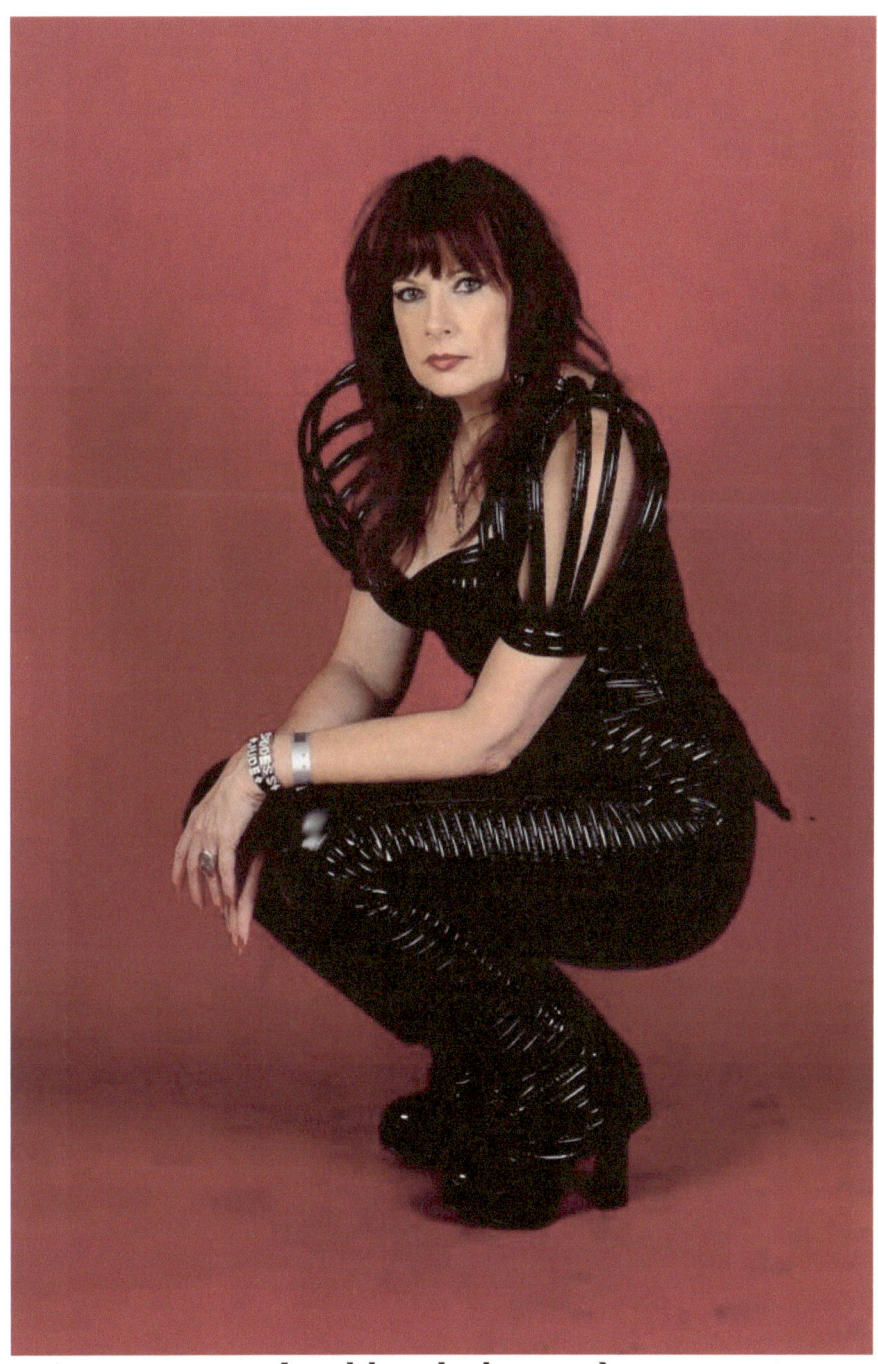

(goddessjude.com)

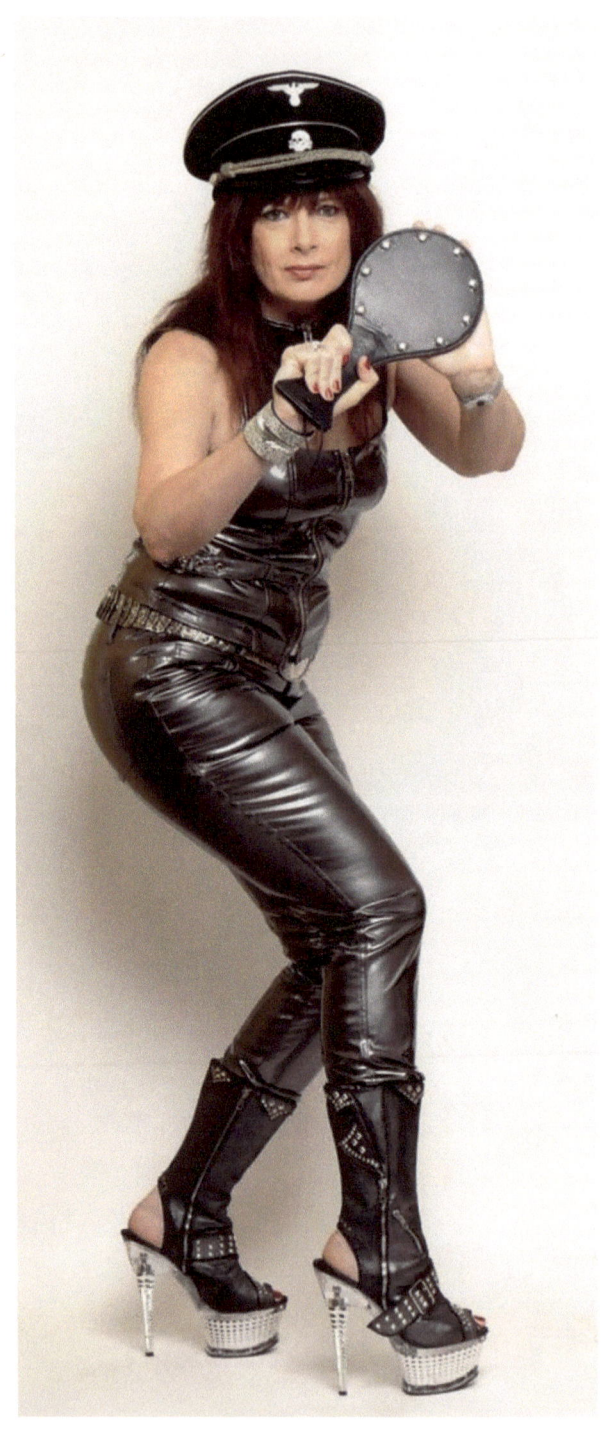

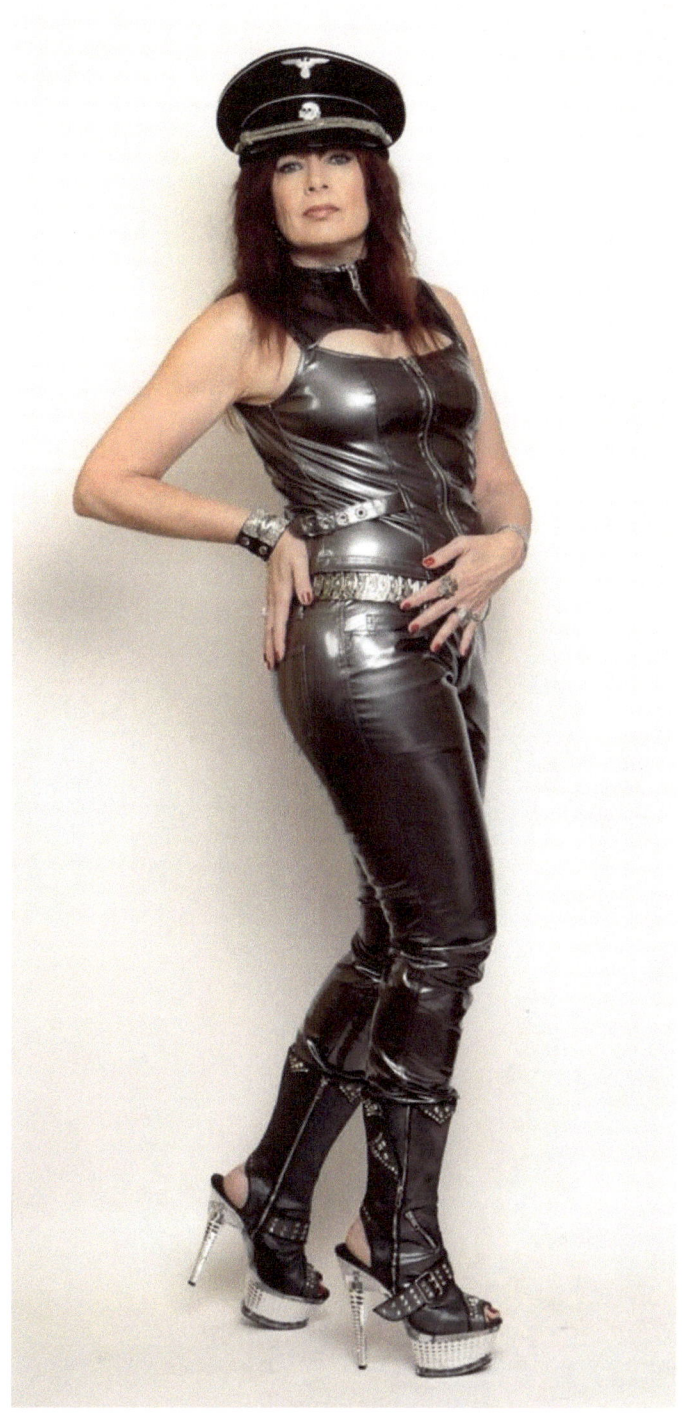

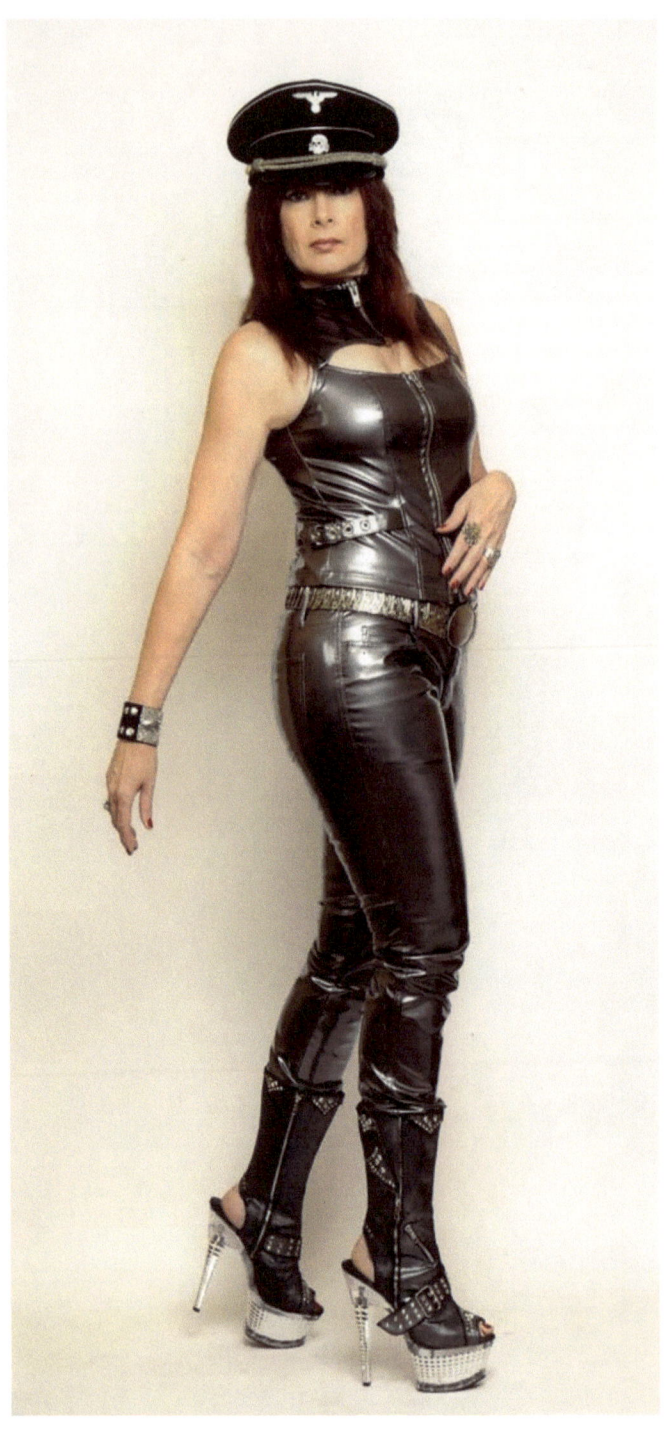

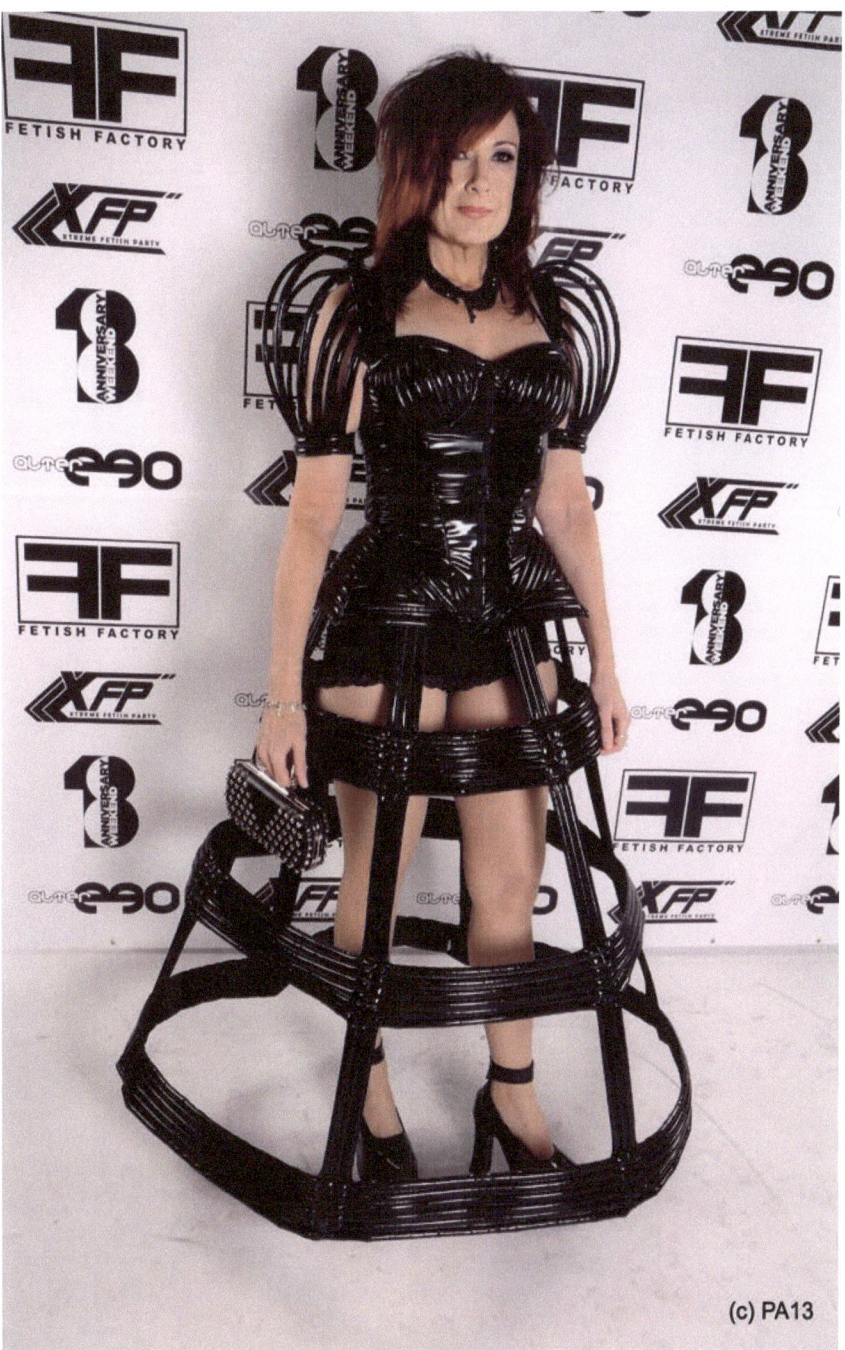

(Goddess Jude 2013)

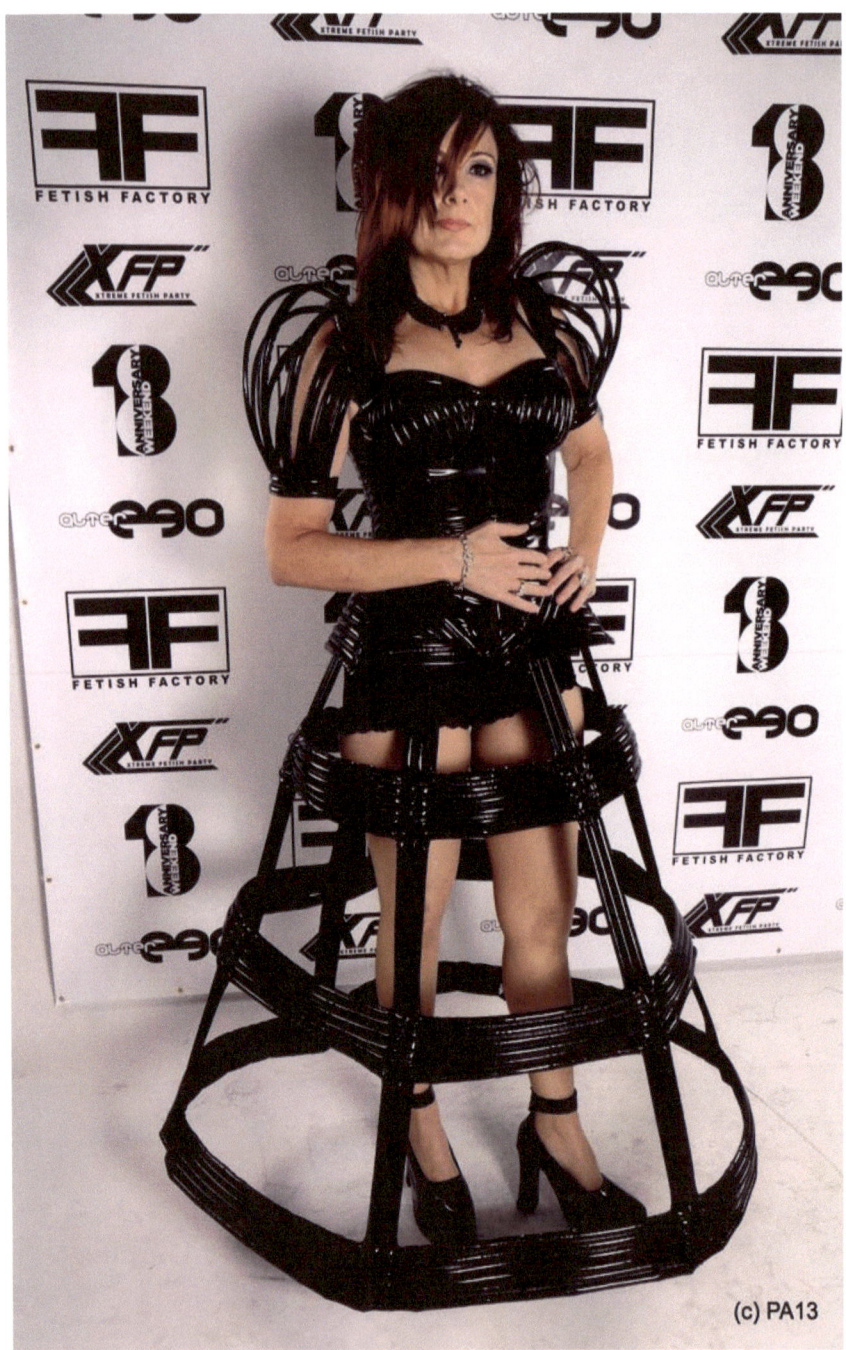

(goddessjude.com)

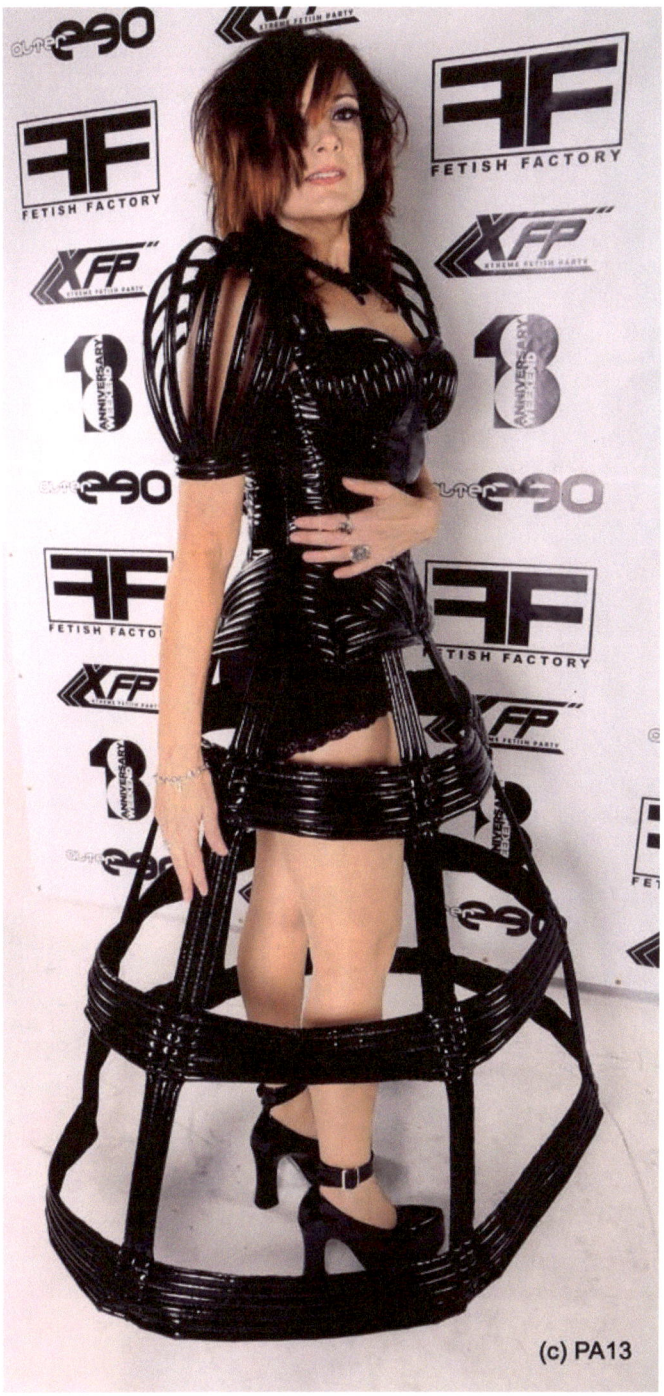

(c) PA13

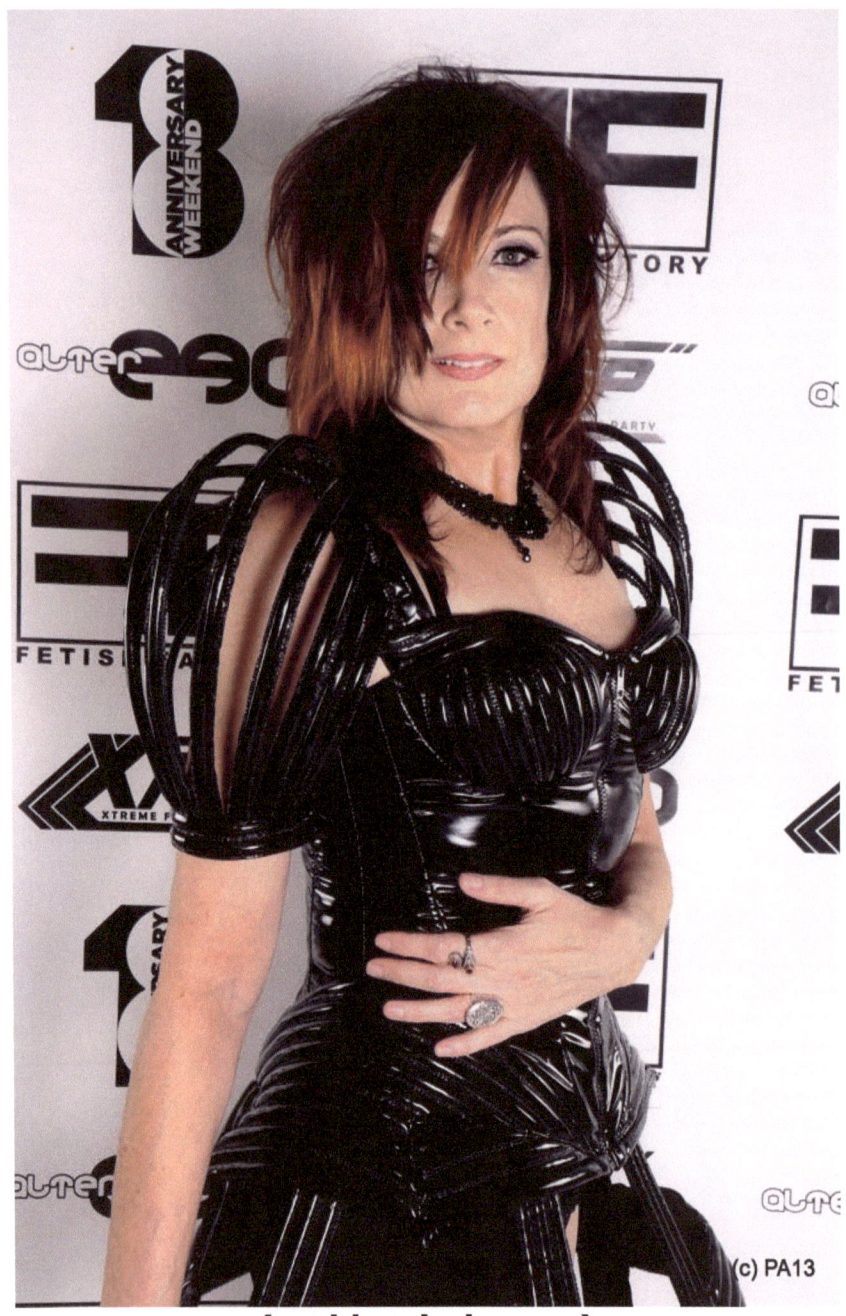

(goddessjude.com)

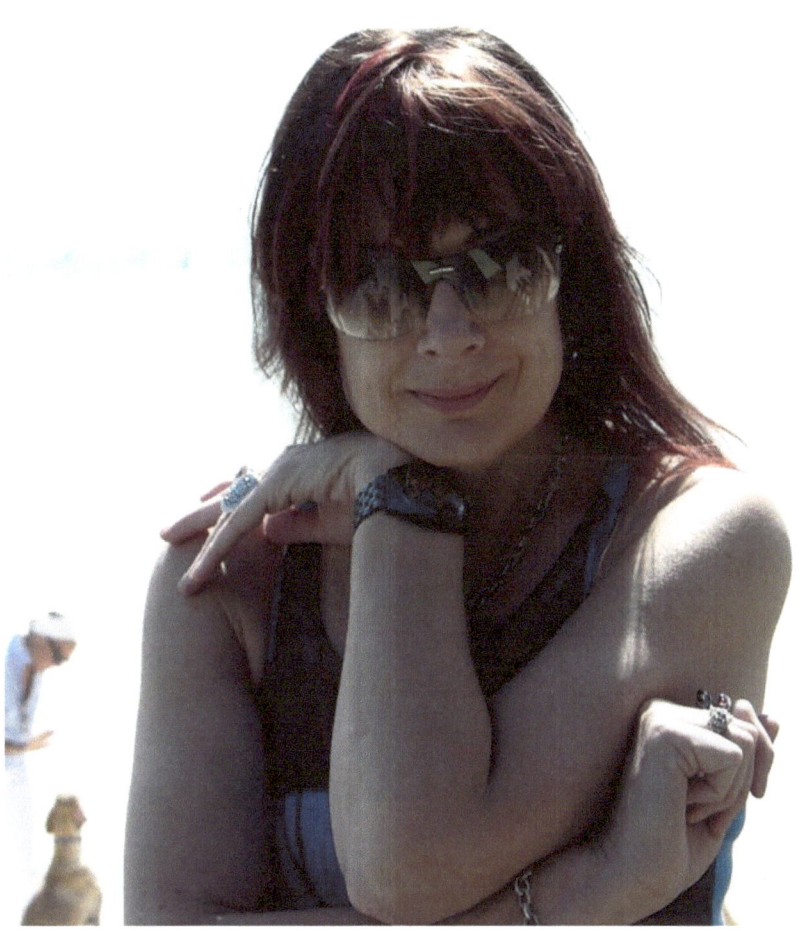

Goddess Jude can be contacted through her website goddess.jude.com

Also Available

Classic American Mistress Volume One: Mistress Porsche Lynn

Available at amazon.com

www.ingramcontent.com/pod-product-compliance
Lightning Source LLC
Chambersburg PA
CBHW040924180526
45159CB00002BA/595